Being Peerless

Being Peerless

Edited by
D.N. Ghosh

JUGGERNAUT BOOKS
C-I-128, First Floor, Sangam Vihar, Near Holi Chowk,
New Delhi 110080, India

First published by Juggernaut Books 2024

Copyright © The Peerless General Finance &
Investment Co. Ltd. 2024

10 9 8 7 6 5 4 3 2 1

P-ISBN: 978-93-5345-523-1
E-ISBN: 978-93-5345-235-3

The views and opinions expressed in this book are the author's own.
The facts contained herein were reported to be true as on the date
of publication by the author to the publishers of the book, and the
publishers are not in any way liable for their accuracy or veracity.

All rights reserved. No part of this publication may be reproduced,
transmitted, or stored in a retrieval system in any form or by any
means without the written permission of the publisher.

Typeset in Adobe Caslon Pro by R. Ajith Kumar, Noida

Printed at Manipal Technologies Limited, Manipal

Dedicated to The Holy Trio

Sri Ramakrishna Paramahamsa
Sri Sri Maa Sarada Devi
Swami Vivekananda

Sri Ramakrishna Paramahamsa (1836–1886)

Sri Sri Maa Sarada Devi (1853–1920)

Swami Vivekananda (1863–1902)

Invocation

चरैवेति चरैवेति . . .
चरन् बै मधु विन्दति चरन् स्वादुम् उदुम्बरम्
सूर्यस्य पश्य श्रेमाणं यो न तन्द्रयते चरन्
चरैवेति चरैवेति चरैवेति

ċaraïvēti ċaraïvēti . . .
ċaran bai madhu vindati ċaran svādum udumbaram
sūryasya paśya śrēmāṇaṃ yō na tandrayatē ċaran
ċaraïvēti ċaraïvēti ċaraïvēti

Aitareya Brahmana, 7.15

The wanderer finds honey and the sweet Udumbara fruit; behold the beauty of the sun, who is not wearied by his wanderings. Therefore, go forward, go forward, go forward.

Contents

Foreword xiii
Preface xxiii
Acknowledgements xxix
Peerless Timeline xxx

1. The Philosophy 1
2. The Founder: Radhashyam Roy – His Life and Times (1899–1932) 9
3. The Beginning: Wading Through Uncertain Times (1932–1960) 21
4. The Architect: Bhudeb Kanti Roy – Growth Through Regulatory Turbulence (1960–1985) 41
5. Business Dynamics 73
6. Interregnum (1985–1987) 81
7. New Protocols, New Experiments (1987–1996) 99
8. The Turnaround (1996–2006) 113
9. Towards a New Model 157
10. The Guiding Light for Future: S.K. Roy (2006–2022) 171

The Road Ahead 181
Notes 186

Foreword

In our indelible days of boyhood, we were familiar with the name *Peerless*. We often saw huge billboards on the streets of Calcutta (now Kolkata) at prominent locations – a discerning image of a human hand dropping a coin into an earthen *Lakshmi Pot*. Much later, we learnt that it was the logo of Peerless Company.

Five years after joining the Ramakrishna Order in 1973, I came to know about Shri B.K. Roy, Managing Director of this illustrious conglomerate. Shri B.K. Roy was the disciple of Srimat Swami Vireswaranandaji Maharaj, the 10th President of the Ramakrishna Sangha. He was also known to Swami Jyotirmayanandaji Maharaj, Monk-in-charge of the Relief section in Belur Math Headquarters. Srimat Swami Atmasthanandaji

Foreword

Maharaj, the 15th President of the Ramakrishna Sangha and the then Assistant General Secretary and Secretary of the Relief Department, had a close bond with Shri B.K. Roy and his family members as a result of their keen interest in relief activities through Swamiji. The growing association of Revered Atmasthanandaji with the Roy family, especially with Shri B.K. Roy, Shri T.K. Roy and Shri S.K. Roy evolved into a deep camaraderie of love, respect and trust. In their admiration for the venerable monk, the Roy family started to regard Revered Atmasthanandaji as their angel guardian. Eventually, all the family members started to receive initiation from Belur Math.

Shri S.K. Roy, the successor of Shri B.K. Roy, and his family used to accompany Revered Atmasthanandaji to various Ramakrishna Ashramas. Initially, I was only formally acquainted with Shri S.K. Roy. As the years passed, I became an assistant to Srimat Swami Atmasthanandaji Maharaj, and the bonding with the Roys also became profound and beautiful. On the auspicious day of Buddha Purnima in 1997, Swami Atmasthanandaji Maharaj was elected as the Vice-President of the

Foreword

Ramakrishna Order, and I was selected as his Secretary. Subsequently, I became closely involved with the Roy family. All the basic requirements of Revered Atmasthanandaji Maharaj, till his *Mahasamadhi*, used to be fulfilled by the Roy family with utmost dedication and humility. Since those days, I started addressing Shri S.K. Roy as 'Roy Saheb' and continue to do so even now. I do not know how and when the Holy Grace of Sri Ramakrishna and Sri Sri Maa Sarada Devi made me a co-pilgrim in the life's journey of this family. It is also true that the Roy family had always been blessed affectionately by Swami Atmasthanandaji.

During the tours of Revered Swami Atmasthanandaji Maharaj to different Ramakrishna centres of India with the Roy family, Roy Saheb always used to prefer staying in a simple manner in the guest houses of the ashramas. Roy Saheb was principally a dedicated family man who enjoyed spending time with his kith and kin. I realized that he was not only the guardian of the Roy family but also a true custodian of the entire Peerless Group. He would listen with great empathy to his employees and become one with them in their joys and sorrows.

Foreword

Roy Saheb's hearty laughter and happy demeanour concealed his fortitude and courage. His medical ailments and physical complications never prevented him from rendering his dedicated services to his employees of the Peerless Group and his family. He had the ability to identify the right man for the right job and assess the situation with a sagacious insight. With determination and diligence, he served the Peerless Group. His strong convictions could transform him into a tough authoritative figure in a challenging situation.

The Roy family's devotional commitment to the Ramakrishna Order has been ranging across three generations now. Therefore, it is natural for the members of the family to be so endearing to the monks of Belur Math. This journey began with:

i) Shri Radhashyam Roy, the founder of Peerless, who was a direct disciple of Sri Sri Maa Sarada Devi. His wife, Srimati Pushpabala Roy, was the disciple of Srimat Swami Vijnanandaji Maharaj, a direct disciple of Sri Ramakrishna.

ii) The second generation of Roys, who were the disciples of Srimat Swami Vireswaranandaji Maharaj, the 10th President of Ramakrishna Math and Mission.

Foreword

iii) The third generation of Roys, who are the disciples of Srimat Swami Atmasthanandaji Maharaj, the 15th President of Ramakrishna Math and Mission.

In his leisure time, Roy Saheb used to speak eloquently on diverse topics – be it his childhood days in Narayanganj (now in Bangladesh), his youth and school days, his later days of hardship in Kolkata or even his professional engagements. I had witnessed his indomitable, tireless efforts to establish the national identity of the Peerless Group.

During his tenure as the Managing Director, he overcame many hurdles and made firm decisions to protect the company. Through his hard work, the Peerless Group showcased by his predecessors has grown to the strength it is today. It was perhaps due to his religious and spiritual heritage.

He was a social person but with a different nature, a visionary industrialist focusing on the common people. He was humble enough to talk to each and every person who crossed his path anywhere. I never saw him tired of resolving his official and family issues.

Roy Saheb was a magnanimous *Karmayogi*. His optimism enlivened others. He was always willing to render any service for Ramakrishna Math and Mission. In his generosity, he even used to donate to several private Ramakrishna Ashramas and other religious and spiritual foundations in India. Seeing everyone happy made him delighted, and he made sincere efforts to make them happier.

He used to provide medical treatment for the middle and underprivileged classes of society through the Group's own dispensaries and medical outlets. He extended financial help for running many charitable dispensaries of the Math and Mission. He had also set up residences for middle- and low-income groups through the Peerless Housing scheme. He arranged for authentic Bengali cuisine in Peerless Inn, Kolkata. He was pleased to launch Peerless Skill Academy in association with Ramakrishna Mission in 2017.

Belur Math, Joyrambati, Kamarpukur, Udbodhan at Bagbazar, Swamiji's Ancestral House,

Foreword

Balaram Mandir, Vrindaban, Kashi, Kankhal and Kankurgachhi Yogodyan were his preferred destinations. He cherished his interactions with any keen disciple of the Ramakrishna Order. Devoted to Sadhu Seva, he used to organize regular *Sadhu Bhandaras* whenever he visited any branch centres of Belur Math. He felt divine bliss in seeing monks partaking in Prasad during *Sadhu Bhandaras*.

Roy Saheb was a rare devotee who offered in abundance without expectations. His source of joy was the happiness of others and he lived for the well-being of others. He internalized the immortal words of Swami Vivekananda, *'Shiva Jnane Jiva Seva'* – service to man is service to God.

In the life of Roy Saheb, we can envision a confluence of four exemplary facets:

1. He was a *Rasoddar* (custodian) to the Sangha like Mathur Babu, the son-in-law of Rani Rasmoni.
2. He was a king like Raja Janak.
3. He was a big-hearted person like Karna.
4. He was a striking example of Swami Vivekananda's teaching, 'Live for others'.

Roy Saheb had established a legacy for the Peerless Group – *'Caraivēti, Caraivēti'* or 'Go forward, Go forward'. He used to nurture some dreams:
1. To establish a college with the idealisms of Swami Vivekananda and
2. To establish a women's college around Joyrambati.

Only after nine years of inception, the Peerless Group became a centurion company. The present leaders of the Peerless Group are carrying the flag of Roy Saheb's legacy. Many obstacles, ups and downs may come on the way for the growth and expansion of the company. However, if the present leaders follow the path shown by Roy Saheb with patience, courage and perseverance, they will surely achieve the pinnacle of success. No doubt, the Peerless Group will grow more and more in the coming years. I am sure one day, Roy Saheb's dream will be fulfilled. The sacred blessings of Sri Ramakrishna, Sri Maa Sarada Devi and Swami Vivekananda may always be bestowed on the Peerless Group's founders and torchbearers.

Foreword

I sincerely hope and pray that the present generation of Peerless Group will carry the Peerless *Lakshmi Pot* with great strength, deep self-confidence, strong commitments, hard work and inner dedication.

May God bless and protect the Peerless family is my earnest prayer.

Swami Vimalatmananda
Adhyaksha
Ramakrishna Math, Yogodyan
Kankurgachi, Kolkata

Preface

Being Peerless narrates the rich legacy of the past three generations in the business of small savings. From becoming the largest non-banking savings organization to diversifying into healthcare, hospitality and real estate, Peerless has a remarkable history that is yet to be fully told.

Marching towards its centenary in 2032, the Peerless Group is evolving on a growth trajectory with a transformed business model for the future. Amid all the substantial changes and hope for progressive growth, the character of Peerless remains unaltered. As this fundamental character unfolds in the warp and weft of time, the new leadership can imbibe lessons to take Peerless to greater heights.

It has been well said by no less a figure than J.R.D. Tata that 'books written on the history of large industrial or business concerns usually suffer from a lack of credibility or reader interest or both.'[1]

To avoid such pitfalls, this book relies on multiple sources, and tries, wherever possible, to reveal the human stories behind the facts and figures. Personal loyalty and commitment to ideals feature as prominently in this story as any drive for profit, and those motivations retain a constant relevance across the years.

But background is equally important. Decisions are only fully comprehensible, and the wisdom of particular actions can only be truly appreciated once the context in which they occurred is correctly laid out. Hence the political and economic history of India is another constant thread in this narrative.

The focus of the book, however, remains closely on the story of Peerless. Amply provided with colourful characters and punctuated by extraordinary events, it is anything but a straightforward tale. Through adversities and personal tragedies, it contains several persistent themes that run like guide rails across the nine decades of the company's growth and development.

Starting with the choice of a name that means 'without equal', the company never hid its ambition to grow. But there was always something more; there was a consistent, broader vision that went beyond the ledger of profit and loss, a vision that touched on larger society and even the Indian nation itself. That philosophy has remained a constant across the company's history, although it has evolved with changing circumstances.

It is this nourishing philosophy that has led the Peerless Group, a corporate entity, to describe itself so often as a family. The full ramifications that come with family status have always been recognized by the leaders of the company, a recognition that has guided its long-term attitudes towards its depositors, agents and employees.

Though the Peerless Group has always regarded itself as a family in a metaphorical sense, at its very heart, there also lies a real family, the Roys. Their story now stretches across four generations and presents a rich and fascinating narrative of close relations, filial piety, respect for persons and traditions and, above all, an overarching sense of service and spiritual fortitude.

The concept of service is very important in the understanding of how Peerless came to be what it is today – a diversified enterprise extended across a wide range of activities, assets and industries. Service in the sense of serving its customers has always been an essential part of the company's philosophy, though this is hardly unique and can be found in many successful businesses. But in the Peerless mindset, the ideal of service goes further. It extends to service to the community, a notion that includes and prioritizes the poorer sections of society.

It also takes in service to the country; the original Peerless Insurance Company Limited, started as part of the Swadeshi movement in the 1930s, was the visible expression of this spirit.

And finally, hidden within service to the community and nation lies a deeper sense of spiritual commitment; service, in a word, to God. The personal piety of the group's founder, Radhashyam Roy, remained a dominant force in his life. His personal links with the Ramakrishna Math and Mission, augmented with his initiation by the Holy Mother Sri Sarada Devi herself, continued throughout his life, and that close connection has been maintained ever since by the Roy family.

Herein lies the core of Peerless because the seeds of its inception were sowed with the blessings of the Holy Mother Sri Sarada Devi, the spiritual consort of Sri Ramakrishna Paramahamsa. At the time of his initiation, she blessed Radhashyam Roy, who had left home to become a monk, saying that he had 'important work' to do, to serve the nation, his motherland.

These themes – service, responsibility, devotion – run throughout the Peerless story and contribute enormously to its richness and its uniquely Indian, especially Bengali, character. The company began life in Narayanganj, south of Dhaka, now in Bangladesh and has remained headquartered in Kolkata since the mid-1930s. Though it grew all across the country, especially in the 1970s, the company's leadership has always stayed a small group and its heart has always been in Bengal.

The Peerless Group was, however, always open to changes, adjusting itself, most importantly, to new technology and to shifts in government policy and the regulatory environment. Yet, over the years, the Roy family has succeeded in ensuring the organization, as it grew to be a conglomerate, never loses its traditions and character and sticks to its roots.

Preface

We offer our *pranams* to Revered Swami Vimalatmanandaji for writing the Foreword of this book. We offer our deepest respects to Late Smt. Lila Deb, the third daughter of Radhashyam Roy and author of *Peerless: A Saga of Expansion from Microcosm to Macrocosm*. We would also like to pay our respects to Late Shri Ajit Kumar Chatterjee (A.K. Chatterjee), the author of *A Peerless Education*. While writing the first draft in 2018–19, Roderick Mathews referred to the abovementioned books, and we express our heartfelt gratitude for his efforts. We also thank our veteran officers for their insights and comments to enrich this book. Subsequently, the original manuscript underwent several revisions and modifications under Dhruba Narayan Ghosh, the nonagenarian editor of this book, who left his mortal frame on 7 November 2023, having served Peerless selflessly until the last days of his life. The editorial team offers reverential gratitude to him for his soulful involvement in this journey of *Being Peerless*.

Kolkata *The Editorial Team*
12 November 2023

Acknowledgements

Revered Swami Vimalatmanandaji
Revered Swami Chidrupanandaji
Late Smt. Lila Deb
Late Shri Dhruba Narayan Ghosh
Late Shri Ajit Kumar Chatterjee
Late Shri Asok Kumar Basu
Shri Deepak Mukerjee
Shri Bhargab Lahiri
Shri P.P. Ray
Shri Asoke Kumar Mukhuty
Mr Roderick Mathews
Shri Pritish Nandy
Shri Partha Sarathi Bhattacharyya
Shri Supriyo Sinha
Shri Bikram Sarkar
Shri Debashish Burman
Shri Pramod Upadhyay
Shri Dibyendu Dey
Smt. Mou Chakraborty
Shri Agniva Kundu

Peerless Timeline

1899 — 11 November, Shri Radhashyam Roy was born

1916 — Shri Radhashyam Roy took initiation from the Holy Mother Sri Sarada Devi

1925 — 30 November, Shri B.K. Roy was born

1932 — 25 October, Peerless Insurance Co. Ltd. founded at Narayanganj, Dhaka

1982 — Golden Jubilee year celebrated

1975 — Swarojgar Yojana launched to eradicate unemployment

1972 — Peerless introduced free insurance benefit against accidental death

1972 — Automatic Promotion system introduced for the field force

1985 — 7 June, Shri B.K. Roy passed away

1990 — Shri S.K. Roy became the Joint Managing Director

1991 — Peerless Hotels Limited was founded

1992 — Diamond Jubilee year celebrated

2023 — PGFI granted the license of Non-Banking Financial Companies – Investment & Credit Company

2022 — 8 May, Shri S.K. Roy, the guiding light of Peerless, passed away

2022 — Shri Jayanta Roy became the Managing Director of Peerless

2019 — PGFI returned ₹1,514 crore unclaimed money to Investor Education Protection Fund (IEPF)

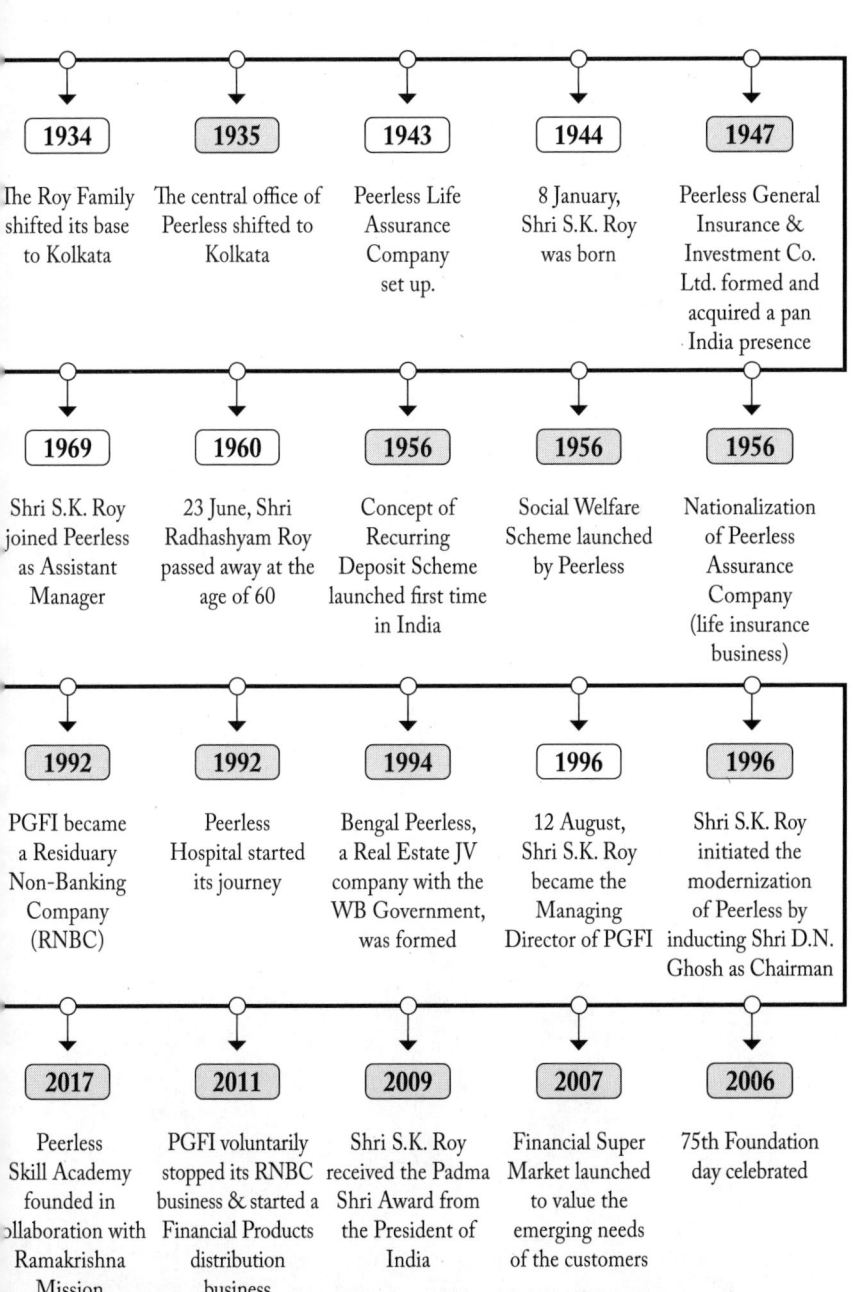

1

The Philosophy

The Peerless story has always been, at its heart, the story of the Roy family. Dynasties are not uncommon in India, where close family ties, even in business, seem especially durable. Where the Roy lineage has proved most consistent is in its ability to maintain an invariable purpose over multiple generations, even among the strains imposed by such enormous growth in the scale of a family business.

This has been the achievement of three remarkable characters, Radhashyam Roy and two of his sons, Bhudeb Kanti Roy (B.K. Roy) and Sunil Kanti Roy (S.K. Roy), who each, in turn, has guided the company to greater success. This has been achieved through a regime of punishingly hard work, combined with an ability to maintain a broader ethical vision while accommodating technological, political and social changes. None of these three men had an easy ride, and all overcame obstacles, vicissitudes and hostility from a variety of directions. There has never been anything easy about the growth of the Peerless Group.

Over the years, the fact that the company has been under the control of a small, dedicated group has proved highly beneficial in responding to the various challenges that have arisen. Flexible leadership has been a key factor, but that flexibility has never been achieved at the cost of the sacrifice of core principles. The original Peerless enterprise was an insurance business, coupled with being a provident savings company, and the enduring stamp that this has left on the psyche of the later corporate grouping is unmistakable. At the very centre of the Peerless empire has been the conception that the money held by the company is not its own; it is held in trust for others, especially small investors; it must be used beneficially and constructively and returned to the society from which it came.

This is an unusual philosophy in business, where the regular model is that the more money taken into the company's hands the better. The idea of

The Philosophy

returning that money usually goes no further than the process of rewarding shareholders or paying employees. From the very start, the Peerless way has been different.

The Peerless attitude to holding and returning money is founded on two ideas. First, this exchange is inherent in the very nature of a savings business, in which money must be returned eventually, with interest. Second, it fits into a wider view of society, which is heavily informed by the religious notion of the unity and indivisibility of all things.

This basic philosophy, which the Roy family has strictly and consistently maintained, dwells on the idea that its members are guardians, trustees or custodians of the wealth they control, not owners who are free to dispose of that wealth for personal gratification. This idea has been sufficiently strong to migrate intact from holding small deposits of individual savers to holding much larger assets, which continue to bring with them a similar sense of obligation. This is why the Peerless Group has been able to diversify its interests so smoothly, from holding small savings accounts to beneficial assets such as hospitals, hotels and housing projects.

Being Peerless

The search for profit and the drive for growth have been as real and as strong within the Peerless Group as in any other corporate entity. The difference is that it has always been tempered with a wider sense of ethical grounding. In its literature, the company will always emphasize that it took on the burden of corporate social responsibility (CSR) years before it had a name, and well before it became obligatory by statute. How much this consciousness of social context has contributed to the company's success is, of course, a matter of opinion, but its constant presence was never in doubt.

The company's outlook and attitudes have always been governed by five guiding core values. These are Resilience, Integrity, Togetherness, Commitment and Performance Orientation, of which three stand out: Resilience is defined as 'the ability to spring back'. Integrity, as 'never letting anyone down', and Togetherness, as 'bonding of Peerless family'.

All five values might be thought of simply as aspects of good corporate practice, but they are not based on any modern management handbook. The history of the Peerless Group shows a long-standing commitment to these values since the company's very beginning, and thus they are not rooted in the teachings of business schools. Where, then, did they come from?

The answer lies in the life experiences of the group's founder, Radhashyam Roy.

2

The Founder

**Radhashyam Roy
His Life and Times (1899–1932)**

Radhashyam Roy was born in 1899 into a respectable, middle-class family living in Narayanganj, eastern Bengal, now in Bangladesh. It was a riverside town dominated by the jute industry, in which his father worked in administrative roles. Radhashyam was a studious and imaginative child, and while still at school, he declared his intention to 'eradicate illiteracy' in India. Such precocious ambition was not confined to education and was similarly manifest in the plans he developed as a young adult. The desire to build independent businesses came to him sometime in the mid-1920s while working as a school teacher. One of his early ideas was to start an independent college in his hometown near Sonakanda Fort, but the plans came to nothing.

Grander schemes soon formed. While performing his teaching duties, Radhashyam worked part-time as an agent selling financial products for foreign-owned insurance companies. He must have shown ability as a salesman because his foreign masters rewarded him with a gold medal, a wristwatch and a sweater, which he continued to use until the end of his life. With the experience and insights he gained, he was able to make realistic plans to start his own financial ventures. He was a clearly a man with innate business acumen, because his new Peerless Insurance Company, which he started with five other partners in 1932, prospered from the very start.

Radhashyam was always attracted to religious ideas and practices from a very young age. He picked up this interest from his father, who was an admirer of Sri Ramakrishna Paramahamsa and a great reader of religious material, especially of a journal *Tattwamanjari*.[1] Radhashyam often visited the Ramakrishna Mission in Narayanganj, close to his home. His daughter, Lila Deb, recollects that while still at school, 'he visited Narayanganj Mission every evening when he would have discussions with the Maharajas.'

The Founder

When Radhashyam was a teenager, Sri Sarada Devi was the *Sangha-janani* of the Ramakrishna Math and Mission.[2] She was the wife and spiritual consort of Sri Ramakrishna Paramahamsa and had survived him; Sri Ramakrishna, who was often simply referred to as Thakur, died in 1886, while Sri Sarada Devi, popularly known as the Holy Mother or Sri Sri Maa, lived on until 1920.

Founded in 1897 by a small group of Sri Ramakrishna's disciples, the Ramakrishna Math and Mission was a vigorous institution. Its leading light was Narendranath Datta, better known under his *sannyasa* name, Swami Vivekananda, and it was he who took the spiritual teachings of his guru to the wider world. The Mission's branch in Narayanganj was only one of many. Its headquarters stood on the banks of the Hooghly, at Belur Math, where a temple dedicated to the memory of Sri Ramakrishna remains to this day, opposite the major temple complex at Dakshineswar.

One day, Radhashyam learned from a teacher at his school that Sri Sarada Devi was still alive and was then further encouraged by one of the elderly sadhus at the Narayanganj mission to seek spiritual initiation from her. He said, 'Go to the Mother. It is the right time to approach her.'

This advice galvanized Radhashyam, who was around 15 or 16 at the time, and he began planning ways and means to travel the four hundred or so kilometres cross country to Joyrambati, where the Holy Mother was living, to seek her *darshan*. At this point he was still at secondary school and living in 'a mess' – some kind of communal hostel. So finding the time and the funds for such an expedition was not a simple matter. Eventually, he came up with a plan.

He waited until his uncle's monthly salary had been paid. Because he knew where his uncle kept the cash, he was able to 'borrow' fifteen rupees; he left a note under his uncle's pillow explaining both his and the money's absence. This may have been a double strategy – to make sure his uncle would not worry about his safety and would also not discover his plan until it was too late to stop him. If that was the intention, it certainly worked.

Radhashyam disappeared unnoticed. But he was not alone. Accompanying him was an older friend, Dhiren Das, who was possibly a school teacher. According to Lila Deb, he was senior to her father in age by several years. 'My father called him Prabhu or master.'

As the evening came to a close and Radhashyam had still not returned to his mess, a search began around the town. When there was no sign of him, an alarm was raised by the beating of a drum. It was only much later that Radhashyam's uncle found the hidden note and realized his plan. Retribution would have to wait upon his return.

This initial triumph – of getting away – was crowned with further success as the two fugitives eventually found the Mother, gained admission to her presence and prevailed upon her to grant them initiation. She was generous and welcoming, though by this time she was in her mid-sixties and not in good health. She suffered from gout, which forced her to adopt the seated pose with outstretched legs that we see in photographs of her.

But Radhashyam wanted more than a blessing. 'The initiation being over, my father sought to be baptized in sannyasa or complete renunciation from the family attachment. The Mother, who was a seer, did not agree to his prayer and advised him, 'Go back to the family for you have to perform **important duties** to the world.'

My father said to her, 'Mother, I have come without the knowledge of my family, and so, how can I chant the name of the Thakur?' The merciful Mother looked affectionately at my father and observed, 'Go back home, and you need not worry. Offer *pranams* only twice a day and that will be enough for you.'

In some ways, this could be seen as a small task; a senior religious figure was making an intelligent assessment of a novice, based on which she decided that, as a teenage runaway, perhaps he was not yet ready to take the momentous decision to withdraw from the secular world. But to the young Radhashyam, this was a life-changing experience.

He had encountered forms of authority before – parents, relatives, teachers – but this time, he had come up against something immeasurably more impressive to him – a representative of the living God, a person touched with a kind of holiness that put her above all others he had known. This was momentous enough, but she then explicitly told him that his conception of his destiny – as a renunciate devotee – was mistaken. She had, in effect, given him a mission to perform important duties in the world, not turn his back on it.

The effect of this encounter cannot be overstated. For a young man with spiritual inclinations, it was nothing less than a glimpse of the divine. But it was also a highly personal piece of pastoral care, or even career advice, for someone earnestly in search of guidance and purpose. To be told by the most revered authority he could consult that he had important work to do in the world was not only a relief, it was a commandment by which to live. Though Peerless had not yet formed in his mind, the courage to mark out his own course through life was undoubtedly planted in him by Sri Sri Maa at that moment.

But the picture was not yet complete. The spiritual aspect of Radhashyam's development may have been determined in his teenage years, but the shape of his secular life formed only slowly over the next decade or so. He qualified as a teacher, then worked in the school in Narayanganj while earning a little extra income as a representative of foreign financial houses – the London-based Prudential Insurance Company and Sun Life Insurance of Canada – learning their business as he went.

This seemingly orderly and comfortable life was suddenly disrupted by a humiliating experience. Lila Deb tells us that her father and a friend both applied for a high post at an office under the British government. 'My father had performed so satisfactorily at the interview that the authorities asked him to see them two days later. He expected to be given the job, but an unpleasant surprise awaited him. My father was rudely shocked to see his friend already appointed to the said post when he went to meet the authorities as scheduled, and very naturally, he felt greatly insulted at the outrageous behaviour of the persons at the helm of affairs.'

This proved to be another life-changing moment. On returning home, he made a vow, 'I shall never serve under anyone, and I shall be doing things in such a way that I will create employment for others and to achieve this goal, I shall try to establish a job-oriented organization.' This attitude, arising out of an injured self-respect, was both defiant and self-reliant. It displayed an awareness of personal self-worth, but it also carried a larger sense of connection to a community trapped in subjection.

The precise date of this humiliation is not known, but its significance cannot be doubted. In the words of his daughter Lila Deb, such thinking had, perhaps, given birth to Peerless enterprise.

3

The Beginning

Wading Through Uncertain Times (1932–1960)

Radhashyam recruited five partners, assembled a working capital of ₹300, and formed the Peerless Insurance Company Limited, which was incorporated on 25 October 1932, based in Narayanganj. This was a time of considerable political turmoil at the height of Mahatma Gandhi's second anti-colonial insurgency. Such a moment might, by some, be considered an inauspicious time to be launching any business enterprise. But the very nature of the new venture – its defiantly independent outlook, its intention to create jobs for local people and its determination to generate wealth beyond the reach of foreign hands – made the moment, if anything, uniquely propitious.

Events proved Radhashyam's timing to be well-judged, and the business thrived from the start. Two strategic choices he made undoubtedly helped its growth. One was his willingness to take very small sums from depositors; low income was not going to be a barrier to its outreach, and in this Peerless could surpass any organization driven by a higher cost base and a need for large profits. The second was his determination to be proactive, to go out and find clients. What later was labelled **'doorstep service'** was part of the company's remit from the start. This allowed it to go further and find customers **beyond the reach of others less adventurous.**

After careful preparation, including long discussions with his friend and former classmate Kali Kumar Chatterjee (K.K. Chatterjee), Radhashyam Roy launched his business career in 1932; India, at that time, was almost devoid of regulation in his chosen areas – running savings schemes, selling insurance and offering banking services.

But that was about to change. Two years later, the Reserve Bank of India (RBI) Act of 1934 created the country's first centralized financial institution, designed to act as a banker to the government, with regulatory powers over banking, currency and reserves. This step was part of a general reform package, the centrepiece of which was to be a newly elected assembly. The idea was that if India was to take increased democratic responsibility for its own affairs, a finance minister responsible to the new assembly would have to be able to control the national economy, a function that would naturally include control of banks, the currency and public debt.

The RBI was not of direct concern to Radhashyam at the time of its inception. The Indian National Bank he had started was still too small to come under its purview, and neither the Peerless Insurance Company nor his other financial ventures were in the business of banking.

Despite the political volatility of the early 1930s and the effects of the global recession that had started in 1929, each of the three of Radhashyam's financial enterprises got off to a good start. The demand for savings and insurance products was high. The bank was the least immediately successful, but overall, business was good enough for Radhashyam to move his headquarters to Calcutta in 1935. Matters changed somewhat with the enactment of the Insurance Act of 1938, a further attempt to regulate the financial services sector. The effect of the Act was to open up competition within the insurance business, and a few years later, in 1943, the company was renamed the Peerless Life Insurance Company Limited.

But conditions were never easy. After the Great Depression, there was a world war and the Bengal famine of 1943, followed by the chaos and riots surrounding Partition. It was then, in late 1947, that the Indian National Bank finally failed. The bank had remained Radhashyam's great hope throughout the twelve years he struggled to establish it, but he was finally forced to admit defeat. Worse, he also had to give up the Jayshree Cinema Hall he had built in Baranagar to repay the deposits he had taken.

Nevertheless, he carried on under the name of Peerless General Insurance and Investment Company Limited. The savings business continued to flourish, and by the mid-1950s, he had enough personal wealth to construct a house in Dum Dum for his large family. But this was the last of his enterprises, for in 1956, in line with the Industrial

Policy Resolution announced that year calling for more state intervention in key sectors of the economy, the government nationalized the life insurance sector, and he lost a large proportion of his business.

According to A.K. Chatterjee, this hit Radhashyam so hard that he considered giving up the business and returning to teaching.

The year 1957 marked the silver jubilee year of Peerless. I doubt very much if the founder or my father was too concerned about the celebration of the event. Peerless was then almost on the verge of liquidation. In 1964, my father vividly described the incident that would have marked the end of Peerless.

The founder thought that all his efforts to keep the company alive had failed and out of desperation he decided to take a teacher's job at a school in Burdwan. One evening, he showed his appointment letter to my father. Two friends sat face-to-face in Dalhousie Square when my father convinced and assured the founder that his destiny was tied up with Peerless.

> The founder tore up the appointment letter and that, to me, marked the beginning of the greatest function to commemorate the silver jubilee of Peerless.[1]

With the loss of life insurance as a field of activity after the nationalization in 1956, the company introduced innovative financial products and widened the range of its activities. However, the Peerless brand would resurrect itself shortly afterwards. Radhashyam did not live to see it. He died on 23 June 1960, even as new products and strategies were being developed by his son.

S.K. Roy sums it up thus, 'Peerless was born out of a desire to serve the nation by creating an institution that would be a bulwark against oppression, against the foreign yoke, against the economic exploitation of the motherland. The founding fathers envisaged creating an institution that would re-dedicate the scattered resources of the economy to the onerous task of nation building, through the economic empowerment of the masses, through the fostering of inclusive growth.'

S.K. Roy also encapsulates Radhashyam's wider personal philosophy, 'The principle of collective action is enshrined in the concept of Dharma propounded in our time-honoured social and religious texts. The vision of Shri Radhashyam Roy, who founded the Peerless enterprise, included not only the creation of an ethical business framework but also the blueprint of an early programme to provide financial and organizational full support to social ventures in diverse fields such as health, education, family welfare and disaster relief. These support programmes also included the active involvement of management and employees in such endeavours.'

Radhashyam speaks to us somewhat at second hand, but his son, B.K. Roy was more expansive about these matters. His brother, S.K. Roy, and his sister, Lila Deb, have described illuminating personal reflections he made that allow us to understand him well.

S.K. Roy recalls, 'I remember something Barda[2] said the day before I joined the company. Even the tea that you are having now is paid for by Peerless. **Remember, Peerless monies are not yours, they belong to the public, and you should join the business only if you are able to safeguard the trust**

with which the public has deposited their monies at Peerless.' This shows the degree to which B.K. Roy took seriously the obligation to safeguard the wealth others had entrusted to his keeping.

His appetite for work was prodigious; a sign hung on the wall of his room that read 'Work is religion'. This was all part of the way he 'dedicated his life to the religion of service'. He seems to have taken this dictum very seriously and acted on it consistently, not just by working hard but also by taking a close personal interest in those he employed.

An old friend once asked him, 'Why do you waste so much time paying attention to the personal problems of so many people?' Gently and quietly, he replied, 'Just see, I may not be able to ameliorate the cases of them all. But they come to me with hopes and expectations, and my lending a sympathetic hearing to them may boost their morale to a certain extent; and thus, I may serve them, I believe.'

This attitude was part of the wider views he held about society and the role of business within it, views that he took directly from an exhortation of

Swami Vivekananda, 'One should serve man with the same intensity as one worships Lord Shiva.' Through all his works, he had been worshipping God, he believed. This chimed in well with several other religiously inspired concepts. Two of these were about the interconnectedness of humanity, though they also appear as a secular philosophy of teamwork – that it is not possible to achieve anything on any scale purely on one's own and that all the Peerless staff were really a family. He observed, 'We all belong to the Peerless family, and the achievements of it are shared by us all.'

Here we can detect the influence of Bhudeb's father and beyond him, the presence of the sages he admired, principally Sri Ramakrishna and Swami Vivekananda. Radhashyam's inner circle of family and friends were all very conscious of his calling as a teacher. He schooled Bhudeb closely both in business and ethics and K.K. Chatterjee's son, A.K. Chatterjee, wrote *A Peerless Education* to record what he had learned from the man he generally referred to as 'the founder'.

K.K. Chatterjee, one of the five partners, was related by marriage to the Roy family. He was just over a year older than Radhashyam. They were classmates at school and remained friends and business associates for life. Lila Deb describes him as the 'intimate friend of my father and our uncle from my mother's side.' Like Radhashyam, he was serious and devout, and the bond between the two men worked to their mutual advantage. Radhashyam had the vision and was always the leader, but they shared ambition and a capacity for hard work.

K.K. Chatterjee's contribution to Peerless over the forty-eight years from 1932 to his death in 1980 is fully acknowledged by the Roy family, and his bust adorns the company's reception area in its Kolkata office, alongside those of Radhashyam and his eldest son Bhudeb.

It was with K.K. Chatterjee's help that Radhashyam also launched three other enterprises in 1932; the Indian National Bank, a film production company called Hollywood Pictures, and a Provident Insurance Company. Again, his ambition was fully on show, and he then hurled himself into the task of trying to make each of the four a success.

The Roy family has made no effort to cultivate a distinct public image and has never courted publicity on a personal level. Its members have participated in many acts of public philanthropy and private charity, but the family has always preferred to remain anonymous.

The principal exception to this is a family memoir, *Peerless: A Saga of Expansion from Microcosm to Macrocosm*, written in the late 1990s by Lila Deb. The original book, written in Bengali, is full of illuminating details about the family's approach to business while giving us an intimate portrait of the family's domestic life. It draws a consistent picture of a family convinced of the virtues of simplicity and dedicated to a kind of traditional, austere piety whose hallmarks include humility, frugality and the idea of duty or higher service.

The book also contains revealing pen portraits of her father and older brother Bhudeb, the men who laid the foundations of the Peerless Group. Both are long departed, and both said little on the public record, but both come to life in convincing ways in Lila Deb's account.

She remembers, 'Our father was grave and composed in nature, and we could hardly approach him with ease. He never indulged in light moments with his children. He would keep himself sitting in a chair at the veranda when we were late in returning home from our schools and colleges. At such an event, to pass by him was as fearsome to us as one feels while attempting to cross a sea.' But the household regime was not unduly harsh or old. 'My mother was soft and mild, and having vested the task of disciplining the children on our father, she could be light and easy with us all.'

The household revolved around her father's regular habits. Lila tells us, 'At 4 a.m., he sat down for his ritualistic meditation, and then at 5 a.m., he roused us all from sleep. The sweet tone with which he awakened us still rings in our ears. He entered our room and chanted the word "Durga" thrice by clapping his palms.'

Again and again, Lila touches upon the central importance of religion in Radhashyam's life, both as a guiding force and as a frame of reference that determined his work, his social life and his leisure. 'My father was the christened disciple of Sri Sri Sarada Devi and he had a deep devotion to Sri Sri Thakur and the Holy Mother . . . Most of my father's friends were the disciples of the

Holy Mother.' His preferred holiday destination was Banaras and his favourite reading matter was *Kathamrita*, a multivolume compilation of the devotional thoughts, teachings and spiritual experiences of Sri Ramakrishna Paramahamsa.

In the last phase of his life, Radhashyam moved house to a new development in Dum Dum, where he lived from 1953 until his death in 1960. During this period, the company went through a difficult time and Radhashyam's health began to fail. 'Due to high blood pressure, my father's health had been causing worries even before changing the residence. The strain of building the company and sustaining its growth through the hard-pressed early days of independent India began to tell. It was noticed that after shifting to our Dum Dum residence my father developed almost a pronounced disinterestedness in life. But here his devotion to religion grew more intense.'

Worse was to follow. The life insurance part of the Peerless Group was nationalized in 1956, and he took the blow very hard. His daughter is unflinching in describing the effect it had on him. She records that it left him 'mentally broken down'.

Through this time of adversity, as ever, he sought solace in religious devotion. 'As a young man, it was his habit to regularly visit the Ramakrishna Mission of Narayanganj in the evening. He would then write down the songs he had heard sung to mother Kali, and on returning home he would himself sing them. He would also play the esraj, performing songs to Sri Sri Thakur and the Holy Mother.'

But his physical strength eventually gave out as his long struggle with high blood pressure took its toll. He endured severe headaches and fits of vomiting and was unable to sustain his accustomed pattern of work. Eventually, he suffered a severe stroke and died on 23 June 1960.

He had fathered eight children – three sons and five daughters – and his eldest son, Bhudeb stepped into his shoes as head of the family. This was not simply a formal role, as the youngest child, Sunil, was still only 16 years old. Bhudeb, or Barda as he was known by the family, also took full control of the Peerless businesses, although he declined to use his father's job title. According to Bhargab Lahiri, a long-serving Peerless employee, 'He described himself as Director and Company Secretary on his business card. This was because his late father was the Managing Director of the company, so he could neither occupy the chair vacated by him nor use his post.'[3] Bhudeb did not formally take up the role of Managing Director until the early 1980s. Such was his respect for his father.

In one revealing passage in his book, A.K. Chatterjee mentions the founder often quoted a saying of Sri Ramakrishna. 'As long as I live, so long do I learn.' This is clearly the mantra of a dedicated teacher, a teacher who is also determined to continue to learn. The author tells us Radhashyam went on to observe, offhandedly, 'He was one of us.' A.K. Chatterjee was not sure what he meant by this at the time but speculated that by 'us' he meant a teacher. Certainly, a large number of those who knew him considered that he saw himself in that way.

But what made him truly remarkable and enabled his passion for teaching to become a mission in business was the interconnections he made between self-improvement, social responsibility, nationalism and religion. He allowed all these concepts to run in a constructive parallel way, thus enhancing their power and appeal. Singly, in the hands of others, these four ideas might become negative or even destructive forces, but in the personal career of Radhashyam Roy and the wider growth of Peerless, they united to bring about a constructive effect.

One early indication of this union of purposes can be found in the young Radhashyam's gigantic ambition to rid India of illiteracy. This was not a goal chosen at random; within it can be seen all the four ideas laid out above. The task, if accomplished, would bring enlightenment and prosperity to individuals and the nation alike. And the benefits would accumulate over time. He understood that reading is the gateway to all kinds of self-advancement, practical and personal, material and intellectual. Though his goal was never fulfilled and still awaited completion, his intuition was correct, and his vision exemplary. The same mindset was carried forward into all that he did.

The company philosophy that resulted has survived remarkably well over the years. Deepak Mukerjee, a director of Peerless, writes, 'Peerless is more than business. It is driven by a mission that aims to give back to the system that nurtures it more than what it draws for its sustenance. This commitment has helped it build, painstakingly over eight long decades now, an impeccable reputation. The ethical standards it has set for itself and its unwavering service to customers and to society at large are well known, as is its ability to reinvent itself with the times and remain relevant for those who have honoured it with their trust.'[4]

This is very well put, but what is remarkable here is not just clarity of expression but the freshness of the thought. It is striking that different employees have slightly different ways of saying all the things conveyed here by Deepak Mukerjee, which powerfully suggests that the philosophy he expresses is real and can, therefore, act as a clear guide to practice.

4

The Architect

**Bhudeb Kanti Roy
Growth Through Regulatory Turbulence
(1960–1985)**

By the late 1950s, Radhashyam was in poor health. Although he had many able collaborators and co-workers, he took a heavy burden of work upon himself, and his physical and mental strength began to give way towards the end of the decade. His eldest son, Bhudeb, B.K. Roy to his colleagues, had been working closely with his father for years; so the change of leadership was not too disruptive. B.K. Roy went on to consolidate the company's standing under a new name – the Peerless General Insurance and Investment Company Limited.

B.K. Roy was destined to enjoy much greater success in business than his father, but his achievements rested very solidly on the work of his predecessor. His sister Lila acknowledges this with regret, and reveals her emotion in a poetic style, noting that it was her father's sheer misfortune that the company he created could not get the touch of golden light during his lifetime.

The son carried on very much in the footsteps of the father, in both his personal style and his approach to business. His sister writes that he had 'a simple and plain way of living' and that he conducted himself with 'gentleness coupled with sublime humility ... He was never deemed only to be a man at the helm of affairs of a business house. His very outfit appropriately projected him with the image of a teacher at a school or college. **His father was an educationist who could instill in his sons and daughters the virtue of humility, which is the gift of education itself.**'

He seems to have perfected the useful ability to be personally impressive while not troubling to exert his authority; he wielded his power lightly. Lila observes that he 'had mastered the art of pleasant speaking' and Professor Ashok Kumar Basu, who translated Lila's memoir from the original Bengali, seems to confirm this. He expressly notes that on first meeting B.K. Roy he was struck by his 'impressive way of speaking'.

B.K. Roy was 'distinctly above the misleading passion of egotism and self-exhibitionism.' Lila adds that his philosophy of life was simple living and high thinking. Like father, like son, 'deep faith in God was his only guide.' We can build up a fuller picture from several further remarks she makes. 'Bhudeb did never pay any importance to emotion.' He believed that 'emotional intensity often did deviate one from the path of carrying out one's duty ... His motto in life became not only to lose himself in his inner self but to look after the interests of all others.' However, she also reveals that 'he never did hesitate to be hard on us if the situation so demanded.'

Here was an austere and disciplined man but one who had a generous heart. Despite the sometimes-forbidding exterior, he could be warm and understanding with family members if they needed guidance or help. He took a special interest in his youngest sibling, Sunil, who was nineteen years his junior and played a father's role to him. When Lila revealed her intention to generate some income to help the family's finances by abandoning her studies for an MA degree that would help her get a teaching post, he forbade it, telling her she need not feel obliged to contribute. He emphasized the need for education, but her sincerity caused him to relent, and in due time, he encouraged her to finish her studies.

One possible reason he maintained such a clear focus on the family and the business was that he never married. According to Lila, this was because he suffered from acute asthma, which varied in intensity with the seasons but which was sufficiently severe to deprive him of sleep. The condition was declared to be incurable and 'he decided not to marry in life', a decision that was 'unalterable'.

When away from his desk, photography and palmistry were his hobbies, and his favourite holiday destination was Puri. Every year he would spend a fortnight there. But his major preoccupation was with his work, and in much the way that it had ground down his father, it took a toll on him too. Lila explains, 'Blood pressure is our hereditary disease. Our father, mother and grandmother suffered from this ailment; and as a natural corollary, Barda too had been suffering from it for a long time; and mental anxiety aggravates it.'

Irreversible kidney damage was diagnosed, but it was too late to be treated. Dialysis was the only way forward unless a transplant could be organized. Bhudeb's brother, Tushar (T.K. Roy), was found to be a match and agreed to donate. But Bhudeb was too weak for the operation, and it was never carried out. He suffered a stroke and died on 7 June 1985.

Professor Ashok Kumar Basu, who knew him well, paid him a fulsome tribute that perfectly captures the mixture of qualities his character contained while emphasizing the tensions that the twin worlds of business and religion constantly imposed on the Roy family.

> It may not be an exaggeration to say that B.K. Roy was an ascetic in the true connotation of the term. In the normal sense, an ascetic is he who withdraws himself from the world of materialism, only to lose himself in deep meditation, in pursuit of salvation. Thus, an ascetic wages a conflict between materialism and spiritualism. But B.K. Roy could compromise between these two. In his inner self he remained brilliantly illuminated with the light of spiritualism where what he did see was beautiful and what he did feel was joy,

pure and unmixed. In his outer world, he was perfectly a man of the earthly terra firma. Here he did devise the most pragmatic ways to boost the advancement of his big business. This too he had done to serve the people and never to service personal interest: by expanding the volume of his business he was able to offer employment to a considerable number of people. **B.K. Roy, to my belief, could execute a happy marriage between materialism on the one hand and spiritualism on the other.**

The new regime at Peerless was very like the old, with B.K. Roy working closely alongside K.K. Chatterjee as Chairman. One major departure was the innovative products on offer. Savings vehicles called *Social Welfare Schemes* were now launched, available to subscribers as 'recurring deposit', a convenient option allowing payment of premiums at the rate of only ₹10, which was ideally suited to those with low incomes. Sales were via 'doorstep service' with agents dealing directly with subscribers in their own homes. Recurring deposit proved to be a popular practice four years after Peerless introduced it in 1956.

The Architect

By 1960 it was not just Peerless that had been forced to adopt new thinking. The central government had its list of concerns for the nascent Indian economy. The government felt the need to act, but it had to balance two conflicting obligations; to encourage savings and investment while also protecting depositors' interests. Its response was to enhance the supervisory role of the RBI, by amending the 1934 Reserve Bank of India Act, adding a whole new Chapter III B. This made the RBI additionally responsible for regulating all non-banking institutions that were receiving deposits, thus for the first time covering the business that Peerless was conducting. From then on, the RBI had the power to regulate all banks, para-banks and savings schemes via legally binding Directions.

The first fruit of the RBI's new powers was a set of Directions in 1966, which created a new category of 'non-banking financial companies' (NBFCs). This designation, as its name suggests, covered all financial businesses that were not banks proper; these already fell under the penumbra of the Banking Regulation Act of 1949, which served as the foundational banking law. Henceforth more and more of the details of running savings schemes were to be scrutinized by the RBI, and this was the area where Peerless increasingly came into dispute with it.

Peerless did well through the 1960s, moving offices from 8/2 Hastings Street to 5/2 Fakir Dey Lane in 1967. Progress was steady. A noticeable change of gear then occurred in the early 1970s, leading to a spectacular rise in footprint and scale for the company. There were several reasons behind this expansion.

One was that, along with its *Social Welfare Schemes*, from 1972, the company offered free accident insurance through a tie-in with the National Insurance Company Limited, a subsidiary of the newly nationalized General Insurance Corporation of India. An already popular product thus became a little more attractive. But the real change was the increase in the size of the sales force, which burgeoned after a new set of conditions were introduced. These included high rates of commission for agents and an automatic promotion system based on sales targets. It was now possible for relatively humble people, many of whom were living in more isolated regions, to make a good living selling a well-reputed product in areas where there was little competition.

A whole new business model was introduced, which proved highly successful. But hidden within this new model were several areas of concern for the regulators. Several incentives and potential conflicts of interest came to their attention. Peerless was repeatedly able to reassure the RBI that the interests of depositors were not at risk, but these reassurances rested to some degree on pleading good character on behalf of the company. The regulators meanwhile had to rightly consider what might happen if some of the relevant practices were adopted by less scrupulous operators.

The Challenge – Part I (1973–1985)

Regulatory and Compliance Issues

To understand the issues that later arose, it is necessary to understand both the business model of Peerless with its rationale and assumptions and the government's justified concerns in some detail.

Being Peerless

The post-1956 Peerless business model was to take small deposits over 10–30 years, invest the proceeds and pay back an agreed sum on a specified date. This is a perfect system, if adhered to. Certificate holders could remain completely secure in the belief that their savings would yield a premium, and that the maturity payment would be made on application. The rate of return was relatively low, but the attractive aspect of saving with Peerless was the company's unblemished record of repayment and the convenience of dealing with its agents in one's own home. Not the most exciting offer on the market perhaps but nonetheless secure and convenient.

It required a large field force of agents, and their remuneration dictated how the model would work. One of the most effective ways to encourage new business was to pay high rates of commission on the first year's deposits; Peerless gave its agents up to thirty percent on the first deposit, later raised to thirty-five percent. In practice, this worked very well to incentivize the sales force, but the fall in the next year's commission to five percent also worked as a disincentive for agents to follow up on existing business, which would be less lucrative for them per hour than finding new subscribers. High rates of commission would likely bring in new business, but it would also cut the company's margins. These two factors would always remain in tension.

However, the greatest challenge within the model was an accounting procedure common within the whole sector, which treated all or substantial parts of the first year's deposit on any certificate as income. Again, in an expanding business, this would present no problems, but in due time it became a serious concern for the governing regulatory bodies. Peerless, with honest intention, spirit and attitude, defended this accounting practice – known as the 'actuarial system' – on practical, theoretical and professional grounds. It was common practice in the life insurance business, as its name suggests, a sector that Peerless had been in for many years.

One criticism of Peerless that turned up later in the court cases with the RBI was that the company did not offer high rates of interest. This was seen as delivering poor value, but this accusation was effectivity playing both sides against the middle. The relatively low rate of return was, in fact, an aspect of depositor protection. The company took meticulous care to place its funds largely in safe investments, primarily with nationalized banks and in government bonds. The company's priority was security, first and always; the deposits were never gambled so that maturity payments would invariably be met. The interests of depositors, therefore, were never in jeopardy.

Much of the regulatory dispute between Peerless and the RBI was really about parties that were not directly involved in the argument. Peerless was trying to do its best within a framework of ideas: to collect money, invest it and repay it. The RBI was rightly concerned about the security of public deposits within such a framework.

There were honourable players within the sector, but there were others less fastidious. The RBI was therefore not always so concerned about what was being done by Peerless, as much as what could be done and was being done by others. By 1980, a scandal – that surrounded the crash of another deposit-taking company that was reported to have defrauded thousands of small investors – amply demonstrated just how ambiguously an apparently similar scheme could be run.

In sum, Peerless could not be duly left off the hook when the rules that it was working under were too loose to restrain operators with rather less in the way of principles. And across the 1970s, those rules began to be made increasingly explicit as the government resolved to investigate and discipline the large areas of the Indian economy that remained informal and opaque.

The first step was the formation of a study group in 1970 under the chairmanship of Bhabatosh Datta, a noted academic and economist. Its purpose precisely was to review the role of nonbanking 'intermediaries'. It was the first body to look at chit-funds, and its view was not favourable. It believed that chit funds 'were not efficient as saving or lending institutions and that they encouraged consumption, spending and in some cases hoarding of scarce commodities.' No action, however, was recommended.

Based on the group's findings, the Reserve Bank of India rightly issued its Miscellaneous Non-Banking Companies (Reserve Bank) Directions in 1973. These Directions set a minimum period for the holding of deposits at six months but no maximum period. It also set a ceiling on deposits at twenty-five percent of the aggregate of the paid-up capital and free reserve of any company; in other words, a company like Peerless could only hold deposits up to a limit of one-quarter of its fixed assets. This would, of course, be a very secure proportion for any depositor, but it also meant that either savings companies could run only very small managed funds or that such a company would need to be very large at its birth to take on even a modest-sized portfolio.

Not for the last time, the evident desire of the RBI to justly drive racketeers out of the sector also revealed a possibility of driving out smaller entrepreneurs, no matter how well-intentioned.

Peerless was adversely affected. While its deposits and liabilities were broadly in line, both were far more than the mandatory proportion of 3:1 of its paid-up capital and reserves.

So, on 14 September 1973, Peerless requested an exemption from the Directions, claiming that it fell outside the scope of the Directions because it was not one of the five kinds of financial institutions that the Directions sought to cover, its business was a special type, it was run on scientific lines and actuarial principles, and because more than ninety percent of the deposits it held were invested in government securities and nationalized banks. The RBI was sympathetic, and by an order dated 3 December 1973, it exempted Peerless from the provisions that stipulated a minimum period of holding deposits for six months, but with certain conditions.

The company was also directed to submit an auditor's certificate every year regarding compliance with the conditions. The exemption was to be reviewed every two years.

On the plus side, the exemption was granted because the RBI accepted that the financial position of Peerless was satisfactory, it was a well-established company, and the certificate supplied by the company's actuarial consultant was supported by data.

Peerless accepted the RBI's conditions and for further security entered into a lien arrangement at this time with a nationalized bank. In 1974, the company also went through another change of name, becoming The Peerless General Finance and Investment Company Limited (PGFI), thus finally dropping the word insurance from its title. The name stands to this day.

Away from the details of regulation, things on the ground were generally going well for PGFI. The company spread across Bengal, with its first branch office in Siliguri, followed by offices in Raiganj, Katihar and Asanol. By 1978, it had an office in Delhi. Peerless also accepted deposits from non-resident Indians by following the rules and regulations to that effect.

In 1974, it also took the opportunity to snap up a well-placed office block in central Calcutta that was being sold off by the Maharaja of Darbhanga. B.K. Roy secured the property at auction, and though the building needed considerable renovation and alteration and he was obliged to take on a number of sitting tenants, eventually 3 Esplanade East, formerly known as the Thacker Spink Building, became a bright, modern office facility – Peerless Bhavan.

The top leadership of the company remained small, with the board of directors never exceeding four members – with K.K. Chatterjee as Chairman, and B.K. Roy and M.R. Mukherjee as ever-present. Meanwhile, the sales pyramid beneath them expanded enormously. Nothing seemed able to stop the growth of the company through the 1970s. The ten-year affordable savings schemes were popular, and through the *Swarojgar Yojana* (Self-employment Scheme), ordinary people could work for the company as self-employed agents to sell its products. Thus, the less-empowered members of society were enabled to earn money in two different ways, while their savings were put to productive use through the parent company's investment in government securities.

In the words of S.K. Roy, 'As the business progressed, B.K. Roy's focus was on three specific areas – marketing, accounting and overall discipline.'[1]

In the short term, this was good news on all fronts, but PGFI's small leadership would eventually prove problematic. The field force also became both expensive and difficult to monitor, while the central staff was increasingly inclined towards industrial militancy.

This tendency flared up in 1977. In that year, as

Peerless employee Bhargab Lahiri recollects, 'An unfortunate incident happened that left a long-lasting mark on the company. A union leader had arrived late and was accordingly marked. It was a simple matter of discipline that was blown out of proportion – all work was brought to a standstill, the management was gheraoed and a section of the employees resorted to distributing extremely derogatory handbills. We were forced to declare a lockout, which was gradually extended to all our offices. The miscreants then shifted their attention to the residence of the Roys in Dum Dum, testing their patience to the very brink.'[2]

There was, however, a silver lining to this cloud. According to Lahiri, 'It was this incident that ultimately led to Peerless opening out-station branches and spreading out.'[3]

Peerless was well placed in 1978 to step forward and use its reach and wealth to ease the plight of millions of people in West Bengal whose lives were devastated by the enormous floods of September that year. Funds were dispensed and, more importantly, practical help was supplied personally by Peerless staff members, senior and junior alike.

But other troubles were looming. The government had been taking an increasingly close interest in the non-banking sector, and the RBI appropriately issued further regulations based on the findings of another advisory committee, set up in 1974, led by Dr J.S. Raj.

Among other things, the Raj Committee recommended a total ban on prize chit funds and similar money circulation schemes. On a plain reading, Peerless was clearly not included under this definition of prize chits as 'the giving of prizes to the lucky ones and the refunding of subscriptions to everyone.'

But the Raj Committee's recommendations produced several official responses.

In 1974, Sections 58A and 58B were inserted into the Companies Act 1956 to regulate companies that accepted deposits more effectively, vast majority of which were non-financial companies. These sections were duly tested in the courts. Later, it was held that Residuary Non-Banking Companies (RNBCs) such as Peerless were outside the purview of these sections.

The RBI eventually, and rightly, issued two

new directions, the Miscellaneous Non-Banking Companies (Reserve Bank) Directions 1977, and the Non-Banking Financial Companies (Reserve Bank) Directions 1977.

Meanwhile, the Parliament also responded to the Raj Committee by passing the Prize Chits and Money Circulation Schemes (Banning) Act, 1978. It was intended 'to ban the promotion or conduct of prize chits or money circulation schemes and for matters connected therewith or incidental hereto.'

Yet even while faced with such a serious legal challenge, Peerless continued to prosper. The financial figures surrounding the company's Golden Jubilee in 1982 were impressive. PGFI had a combined workforce of 350,000 agents and field officers, with around 3,000 permanent staff manning 75 offices around the country who serviced around twelve million certificate holders. Profit after tax for the year was ₹4.29 crore, while paid-up capital and reserves stood at ₹3.7 crore. The company also held over ₹325 crore in government securities.[4] Peerless became recognized as the largest RNBC in India.

This reflected not only the enduring popularity

of the *Social Welfare Savings Schemes* and the good standing of the company in the public eye but also the introduction of new technology within the company's administrative structure. B.K. Roy had taken a keen interest in computers from the early 1970s and finally introduced their use in 1980. In this he relied heavily on the 'domain knowledge' of S.R. Mukherjee; **Peerless had one of the first five computers in the country**.

But not everything was rosy. A further application for exemption under the Banning Act was refused by the Reserve Bank on 19 March 1980, after which the government of Madhya Pradesh served its notice on Peerless under the Act on 1 April 1980. This too was deferred by the court.

It placed the RBI's genuine concerns very squarely in the public domain, and the press moved in on the story. An article that appeared in a leading magazine dated 30 April 1983 mentioned that 'the Calcutta-based Peerless, now the largest non-banking savings company in the country, is under attack from a formidable trio: the West Bengal Government, the Reserve Bank and the LIC, with even the Central

Government, now beginning to take interest in the matter.' The piece also conceded that 'on paper, Peerless's claims sound [sic] very good.'

But the general criticisms were that Peerless returned a low rate of interest, its system of accounting undervalued the company's liabilities, the agent's commissions were too high and many certificates were lapsed or discontinued by default of payment.

B.K. Roy insisted that there was no provision that stood in the way of the company's present style of operations and that the conditions of the savings scheme were agreed upon with the client at the start. 'Are our depositors fools that they should come flocking to us with their money if they thought that their savings would be lost, or that we were not being fair to them?' he asked.

He felt the article was not balanced, and wrote a long letter to the magazine, which was carried on 15 June 1983.

'Your report mentions about the lapsed certificates but fails to point out that the company offers many incentives for the continuation of certificates including the special facilities for reviving a certificate, even without payment of arrears. Finally, the certificate holders' money is absolutely safe since their funds are invested entirely in government custody. All these are fundamental differences between Peerless and other non-banking savings companies.'

This was not just a public front. B.K. Roy felt entirely justified in the company's policies. In a letter to A.K. Chatterjee, dated 23 August 1983, he wrote:

> We have been treating the first year's subscription as income and all second and subsequent years' subscriptions are credited to the certificate holders' fund. This fund, together with the compound interest credited to it every year, will be more than sufficient to meet any kind of contractual liability to the certificate holder. Therefore, even after spending the first year's subscription, the company is in a commanding position to meet all its liabilities to the certificate holders. The procedure has been followed by the company for the last 25 years or so and the company has also paid taxes on that basis.

Being Peerless

The innate strength of character that B.K. Roy showed was rooted in the integrity of his actions, a quality that was inherent in his father too. B.K. Roy foreshadowed most of the main arguments that were heard in court over the subsequent years. Some stood and some fell; some were outflanked by subsequent Directions from the RBI.

But he did not live to see them tested and hear the verdict of the Supreme Court in favour of Peerless in 1987. His health gave way before the first legal battle between Peerless and the RBI was resolved. He was diagnosed with serious kidney damage and at the age of fifty-nine, he was considered too old and too weak to undergo major surgery. A trip to Guys Hospital, London, in 1984 saw no improvement, and he eventually died in Calcutta on 7 June 1985.

Praise for B.K. Roy's achievements and his character have never been in short supply.

S.K. Roy has paid him many fulsome tributes over the years, but he has also placed him accurately within the history of Peerless. 'The opening partnership was between my father Radhashyam Roy and K.K. Chatterjee; they were not only inseparable as friends from school but also the founding fathers of the organization. The partnership between B.K. Roy and M.R. Mukherjee was equally important and has left an indelible mark on the history of Peerless, which has always sought to embrace the new, whatever the cost may have been.'[5]

Certainly, B.K. Roy had a long record of successful innovation and a pioneering spirit. **He made Peerless the first company to introduce recurring deposit and then to give free accident insurance. He introduced direct marketing through *Swarojgar Yojana*. He devised the automatic promotion system for agents,** which gave a dramatic boost to sales and was an early adopter of computerization. He was also proud to claim that his policy of heavy investment in government securities was adopted by the RBI as a norm for non-banking finance companies.

His motto was '*Bahujana sukhaya bahujana hitaya cha*' (For the happiness of the many, for the welfare of the many), and one Peerless insider,

Parimal Kanto Das, has illustrated his simple abstemiousness with telling intimate detail. 'B.K. Roy presided over an empire that was valued at more than ₹1,800 crore but had only ₹20,000 in his own bank account.'

B.K. Roy and his colleague K.K. Chatterjee continued what his father strictly adhered to during his lifetime. A.K. Chatterjee narrates how, four years after Radhashyam's death, Bhudeb and K.K. Chatterjee commuted to work like any ordinary office worker. When A.K. Chatterjee came home in 1964 after living in London for several years, he 'found that the company was thriving and the company could easily afford cars for my father and the founder's son. But they were then using public transport, first, a train to Sealdah, then a bus from Dalhousie Square to 8/2 Hastings Street.'

B.K. Roy did not give up his frugal habits. Asoke Kumar Mukhuty, the company's long-serving chief financial officer, remembers, 'He always used to tell us that we are custodians of public money. So, whenever he visited Bombay, Delhi, or elsewhere, he never stayed in expensive places. Although he had the means to stay in a five-star hotel, he didn't.

In Bombay, he used to stay at the Windsor or Astoria. Somewhere in the three-star category. He used to stay very moderately.'[6]

His sensitivity to matters of expense extended to the customers too. According to Bhargab Lahiri, 'B.K. Roy told us that any building we take on, to buy or rent, must be near a bus stand, a station or a bank.' This was for easy access and convenience of the company's clients. 'He applied these criteria when he acquired Churchgate Chambers in Mumbai.'[7]

But above all, Mukhuty remembers one characteristic feature about him. 'He was a man of commitment, whatever it was.' And he illustrates this through an anecdote:

> He used to come into the office at 1 p.m., and stay till 9–9.30 p.m. But from 8 a.m. to 12 noon, he would plan and do other office work at home. One day, he told me, 'Tomorrow, I will give you 110 certificates.' He was the one who signed on depositors' certificates. That particular day, when he left the office, he had forgotten to sign. When he got home, he realized that the next morning

they could not be paid without his signature. So, after dinner, he came to the office to sign. He came back just to do that at 1 in the morning.[8]

In 2014, S.K. Roy wrote, 'While we discover new ways and means of doing business, we still remember to stay accountable to society. Peerless always lends a helping hand to those in distress including victims of natural calamities, the sick, the elderly and the needy. **The Peerless Group firmly believes that profits and principles must go hand-in-hand.**'[9]

Dynastic succession has its advantages and disadvantages. Large families can sometimes breed intense rivalries rather than loyalty, while small families naturally restrict the amount of talent available. When family ties are secure, stability has to be traded off against stasis – excessive respect for elders and traditions. Any successful dynasty has to navigate these extremes, and the Roys are a good example of how to do this.

Family members have brought forward their own distinct abilities within a changing business environment, and have found ways to maintain constructive motivation within a constant set of guiding principles. And in turn, leading members of the family have exhibited a consistent ability to choose good advisors and recruit talented executives, an ability that has proved absolutely crucial in maintaining the success of the company. It has also populated its history with interesting and capable characters.

5

Business Dynamics

Originally in the 1930s, the main difficulties facing the company were the typical problems of any young business – finding a niche, building a client base, establishing a reputation, setting up standard practices and dealing with competition – with the added difficulty of doing all this under a colonial regime, at a time of global depression and local political instability. When the company took its first steps in late 1932, Mahatma Gandhi's civil disobedience campaign had entered its second year. The man himself was languishing in jail, recovering from the 'fast unto death' that had brought B.R. Ambedkar to conclude the Poona Pact in September 1932 concerning the representation of the 'depressed classes' in the proposed new assemblies envisaged under a British reform package, eventually enacted in 1935.

The company rode through this initial turbulence without serious difficulties but was forced to enter a new market environment with the passage of the 1938 Insurance Act. This regulated the Indian market in insurance products but also exposed Peerless to new competition. Further difficulties arrived with the outbreak of war in 1939 and eventually with Partition in 1947, which cut the company and many of its employees from their roots in East Bengal, now part of the new state of Pakistan. This was a cultural and emotional blow, but it was also a material handicap as it severed the company from a large part of its established client base.

Independence was joyfully welcomed, but free India did not offer great new opportunities for the Peerless Group. On the contrary, from 1947 onwards the most serious challenges to the group came from the government, at both central and state levels. This was partly a question of ideology; the new political regime introduced a socialist imperative into the Indian economy and with it, an outlook that did not look favourably on privately owned financial operations like Peerless. The government also faced the daunting task of building an entirely new administrative and regulatory framework almost from scratch, and as this slowly emerged after Independence, the freedom for financial companies to act was increasingly restricted. The first significant result of this new environment was the nationalization of life insurance companies in 1956. This placed a large portion of the Peerless enterprise in public ownership, which came as a heavy blow to Radhashyam Roy.

By the early 1970s, the company was well-placed to begin a long period of sustained growth, and it expanded relentlessly through the next decade. It moved its offices to its current location in central Kolkata in 1973 and began a conscious effort to reach further into parts of the Indian interior that were ill-served by banks and post offices. The company became a formidable structure, employing thousands of field agents and offering savings opportunities to millions. Both of these processes were fully in line with the company's central philosophy – to help the poorest to help themselves.

Peerless enjoyed spectacular growth. By the time of its Golden Jubilee in 1982, it was acknowledged as the largest non-banking savings company in the country. This rise to prominence was a great boon to many, but it also brought Peerless to the attention of several large institutions, which suspected its motives and wished to investigate its practices.

In 1978, the government rightly attempted to regulate certain aspects of the informal financial markets within the country with the passing of the Prize Chits and Money Circulation Schemes (Banning) Act. The activities of Peerless did not obviously fall within the ambit of the Act; for the most part, Peerless sold and administered savings plans related to insurance products, and did not run speculative money circulation schemes. But this did not deter the government of West Bengal, then run by the Left Front, newly elected in 1977 – ideologically opposed to the private financial sector – from initiating proceedings to close down the Peerless operation, using the Banning Act as a pretext. Peerless contested the action vigorously, and a long legal battle continued right up to a Supreme Court ruling in 1987 when a full bench decided in favour of the company.

This ruling arrived too late for B.K. Roy, who died in 1985 struck down by a combination of high blood pressure and organ failure at the age of sixty, the same age as his father. The loss of Bhudeb Babu was in itself a heavy blow for the company. Unfortunately for the company, the early eighties saw the cumulative loss of many experienced figures: K.K. Chatterjee, the childhood friend and original partner of Radhashyam, who had been the company's chairman since 1960, and H.K. Sen, who succeeded K.K. Chatterjee. The conspicuous absence of the three stalwarts seriously disrupted a company that had always relied on a small, close-knit leadership group. The company was forced for the first time to seek outside management candidates.

6

Interregnum

(1985–1987)

Companies are not inanimate objects. They are guided by human minds and propelled by human energy.

The evolution of the Peerless Group serves as a classic example. As the company branched out far and wide across the country, its leadership always stayed small and focused, allowing coherent direction to combine with the force of a mass movement. This was not an easy process or a comfortable alliance. There was a loosening of leadership focus for a decade after the death of B.K. Roy in 1985, and maintaining such a large network of field agents proved problematic, both in terms of administration and incentivization. But the way these problems were solved can serve to highlight the positive roles that individuals played in the Peerless story.

With the new professional management, Peerless entered a phase of expansion and diversification but at the same time was beset with confusion and controversy. The ownership of the company was transferred and retransferred, and a long legal battle with the RBI – the country's chief regulatory body for financial institutions – over certain aspects of the company's business practices continued for several years until 1996.

The growth of Peerless under B.K. Roy's leadership was truly spectacular. By the time of his death, the group was the largest non-banking financial company in India. It had millions of certificate holders, a formidable asset base and an infrastructure that extended the company's reach to all parts of the country. But unlike the smooth transition from father to son in 1960, B.K. Roy's death in 1985 threw the company into a period of uncertainty. At the time, B.K. Roy's youngest brother, S.K. Roy, was not willing to take the central role that his brother had played. He held back, prompted by a mixture of natural modesty, consciousness of his own inexperience, and a record of ill health. There was Tushar, his elder brother, but he had not often been closely involved with the business; he had separate interests in engineering.

The loss of B.K. Roy plunged the Peerless Group into crisis, for although the company's financial position was strong and growing stronger, it came at a particularly unfortunate time for the company on two fronts. Firstly, the legal challenge from the RBI continued to hang over the company's future; important decisions still needed to be made. Secondly, and rather more seriously, there was no immediate successor to take on the dominant leadership role that B.K. Roy had played. His knowledge of the business was unparalleled, and his experience, ingenuity and judgement would be hard to replace.

The burden of decision and leadership fell on S.K. Roy, but he faced an immediate challenge to his authority. At that time, the company's chief agent, who had become wealthy through his work for Peerless, demanded a senior role in the management. He mobilized the company's field force and conjoined his own grievances with theirs. The police had to be called in to control the agitation. With negotiations, the frenzy subsided but discontent persisted among the workforce.

Facing such hostility, S.K. Roy appealed for help to the wider family networks that surrounded the company. The first to respond was Tushar. From early 1986, he helped his brother with the management and direction of the company. S.K. Roy also approached the sons of K.K. Chatterjee asking them to join the board. But owing to a variety of reasons, of the four, only Asis Chatterjee was able to make himself available.

S.K. Roy was very conscious of the scale of the task he faced. He had become a fulltime director of the company in 1983 – a position he took seriously enough to swear an oath dedicating himself to the role. He had been with Peerless since 1968. He knew the business very well. S.K. Roy felt that the company should be put into professional hands, and he set out to find management talent adequate for the task. The year 1986 proved to be a no less traumatic year.

First, the long-awaited prize chit case finally came to court. The whole existence of Peerless was back in balance. On 14 March 1986, a single judge in the Calcutta High Court ruled that the company's activities did fall within the Banning

Act of 1978. This was a potentially mortal blow, but it seemed to fly in the face of the law as plainly written. Peerless had never offered prizes, and the agreements over the deposited monies were all singly made and not communal. Nevertheless, if the company's endowment schemes were ruled illegal, its business would be instantly defunct.

An appeal was the only way to save the company, but a decision had to be made whether to take it up to the Supreme Court or whether to leave it at a lower level in Calcutta. This latter course was deemed more tactically wise, so the appeal was duly lodged.

On 23 May 1986, a Division Bench of Calcutta High Court reversed the single judge's decision and ruled in favour of Peerless. Any jubilation was, however, short-lived, because the RBI then justifiably counter-appealed, and the whole matter was sent up to the Supreme Court for a final verdict.

Meanwhile, sections of the Peerless administrative workforce had become unruly, with a list of varied grievances. A report by the management dated 14 June, revealed that the problems arose from a combination of union militancy, uncertainty over the company's future in the light of the continuing court case, concerns about potential nationalization (which some in the government of West Bengal had been calling for) and complaints about the chaotic management of staff transfers.

There was further bad news. H.K. Sen, Chairman of the Peerless Board since 1980, unexpectedly died on 2 June 1986. This fell as a last straw for S.K. Roy, who felt unable, with only two years' top-level management experience, to take the situation forward. A.K. Chatterjee, who was on a prolonged stay in Calcutta at the time, and lived through this period in very close contact with S.K. Roy, writes, 'After the death of Bhudeb Babu, Sunil felt as if he was trying to sail through an uncharted ocean in a rudderless boat to reach an unknown destination. He had very few people to turn to.'

As a last throw of the dice, on 30 April 1986, S.K. Roy wrote to all the shareholders asking them either to become directors or to nominate suitable directors. None stepped forward.

Extensive changes followed. The company ran an advertisement on 10 July 1986 in *The Statesman* in Calcutta, *The Times of India* in Bombay, *The*

Hindu in Madras, and *The Hindustan Times* in New Delhi, seeking an experienced chief executive. S.K. Roy also moved to restructure the board of directors.

Four names were then shortlisted from twenty promising candidates for the executive position. Of these four, the strongest seemed to be the fifty-four-year-old Prasanta Chandra Sen (P.C. Sen), who had a long career of high-level management in publicly owned companies behind him and was then the CEO at Burn Standard. There was a problem with his immediate availability, but the obstacles were negotiated, and he was appointed Managing Director in August.

He was no stranger to Peerless. He was the son-in-law of the late H.K. Sen, having married his only daughter. Indeed, P.C. Sen was something of a facilitator. Besides his ties with Peerless, he had extensive links within the Bengal business community.

But despite all the good intentions, this new lineup was in for a turbulent few months. Within days of taking up his new appointment, P.C. Sen felt the wrath of the workforce. There were pickets camped outside the Peerless headquarters on Esplanade East and, in their zeal to make their case, they physically assaulted him and did sufficient damage for him to be hospitalized.[1]

But soon Peerless, without any partners, was back in control over its own destiny and with an experienced and highly ambitious chief executive in place.

This was a turning point for the company. It had tried to develop beyond the bounds of family but the transition had proved difficult. And although the moment was heightened emotionally by the death of two key leadership figures, there were two wider issues coming to a head at this time.

The first was that Peerless had simply become too big – too big for the regulator to ignore and too big to continue in the model it had set up and run successfully. The RBI had still not fully worked out what to do with the company, and the resort to law in March 1986 was the best it could manage. It had been clear from the late 1970s that the classification used by the RBI did not have a neat space for Peerless. Publicly, Peerless was described as RNBC – the largest in the country. But going by the rules, Peerless did not fit into the formal rules governing the conduct of RNBCs.

This opened the field for other candidates to come forward, and the family decided to put the company into what was called 'professional management'. Ten years of growth followed, but in the short term, there were periods of instability, and over the longer term, there were poor investment decisions that began to affect the company's cash position. The leadership issue was eventually resolved in 1996 when S.K. Roy took sole charge of the company and brought in a new team of expert managers. The investment portfolio and balance sheet issues took much longer to repair, but the recovery was completed by 2006.

The Challenge – Part II (1985–1987)

Regulatory and Compliance Issues

In its first set of directions of 1966, the RBI used a fivefold definition of a Non-Banking Finance Company as any company engaged in hire purchase finance, housing finance, investments, loan equipment leasing and mutual benefit business. By

1977, the Reserve Bank Directions had expanded this list to eight categories, as any business that was not: an equipment leasing company, a hire purchase finance company, a housing finance company, an insurance company, an investment company, a loan company, a mutual benefit financial company, or any that was not 'a miscellaneous non-banking company'.

This was hardly satisfactory and indicated that 'the official mind' was finding it very difficult to deal with businesses in the informal sector. This had been a problem from the very start, and in 1966, when clear definitions were first sought, the officials in charge of drafting the regulations left themselves a get-out clause.

At the same time, S.K. Roy was confronted with the uncomfortable truth that Peerless was an unwieldy creation within its original business model, and there was no obvious way forward into expansion without a major restructuring of the company, its procedures and its leadership structure.

The appointment of P.C. Sen and the merger

with a well-known conglomerate was an attempt to resolve all of these problems. It might have worked, but a combination of personalities, contingencies and timing meant that in the end Peerless had given away too much and gained too little. The eventual outcome, that S.K. Roy bought back his shares and that P.C. Sen stayed on as Managing Director, meant that Peerless could begin to refashion itself by expanding into traditional business ventures while maintaining harmony in the boardroom.

This could, in historical terms, be called a new version of Peerless – a company with a professionalized executive leadership, cognisant of its size in capital terms, willing to adapt to current business conditions, moving away from small depositors and fully aware of the changing regulatory environment.

Finally, the appeal came up in the Supreme Court. This was the moment of truth.

To lose at this point would be to lose everything. The last eighteen months had seen grief, turmoil and tension. Whatever could be retrieved from this period would be determined by the verdict. To lose would probably mean the end of Peerless in any recognisable form.

Some kind of nationalization might follow, with perhaps the return of all deposits to certificate holders and mass redundancy.

Peerless was the respondent in the case and was represented by the veteran Communist parliamentarian Somnath Chatterjee. He was an impressive performer who supported his case very thoroughly by unpicking all the arguments that had been produced to equate a Peerless Endowment Scheme with a chit fund. He also touched on the dire social consequence that would result if the company had to be wound up.

There were lighter moments too. Bhargab Lahiri remembers that the Court had wanted to understand Peerless's business thoroughly and had asked for details of the very large body of field agents the company claimed to have.

'The judge advised us to give the names and addresses of all those agents, including senior inspectors, area supervisors etc. We had to purchase four big trunks to put the papers in, and we carried them into the Supreme Court. The judge asked,

"What is in here?" We said, "You wanted names." He waved us away. "Put it elsewhere. I don't want to see. I am withdrawing my order".'[2]

Finally, the long-awaited, twice-disputed decision was delivered on 22 January 1987.[3]

Honourable Justice Chinnappa Reddy started his judgement very clearly, pinpointing the central question in the case. He asked, 'Is a Prizeless Chit a Prize Chit?' He accurately described the terms and conditions of the standard Peerless endowment savings scheme, then asked, 'What is in its nature?' In answer, he declared, 'It is not a gambling scheme. It is not a lottery scheme. There are no prizes, no gifts, no elements of chance.' He continued, 'The Legislature did not intend to so expand the meaning of prize chit as to take in every scheme involving subscribing and refunding of money.' Referring to the Banning Act, he then made the crucial declaration, 'The definition of "Prize Chit" expressly excludes the conventional chit obviously for the reason that the "chance" element is overshadowed by the "certain element". Section 2(e) of the Act does not contemplate a scheme without a prize, and therefore, the endowment certificate scheme of the Peerless Company is outside the Prize Chits and Money Circulation Scheme (Banning) Act, 1978.'

This was a victory in no uncertain terms, and the logic was so clear that it raises the question of why a single learned judge in March 1986, and all the legal brains available to the RBI for six years, had thought it could be otherwise. The central point was established. The main business of Peerless was legal, and the company would be able to carry on.

This was, of course, a great relief, but many questions were raised – on agent commissions, the steep drop-off in subscriptions after the first year, the actuarial accounting method, the terms of forfeiture and the level of return. These were balanced against recognizing the capital adequacy of the company and its 'satisfactory financial position', approving of the social benefit that arose from its promotion of the habit of regular saving among ordinary people and noting its good record of repayment on maturity.

But viewed from the bench, the wider picture was much darker. The judgement contained multiple warnings about the vulnerability of the

Holy Mother Sri Sri Sarada Devi at Joyrambati, West Bengal

The Peerless Trinity
Shri Radhashyam Roy (centre), Shri B.K. Roy (right) and Shri S.K. Roy (left)

The founder of Peerless, Shri Radhashyam Roy, and his wife, Smt. Pushpabala Roy

Shri Radhashyam Roy overseeing a gathering of monks and devotees at his home in Dum Dum, Kolkata

Shri Radhashyam Roy

Shri K.K. Chatterjee

Shri B.K. Roy

Shri M.R. Mukherjee

Shri S.K. Roy

Shri D.N. Ghosh

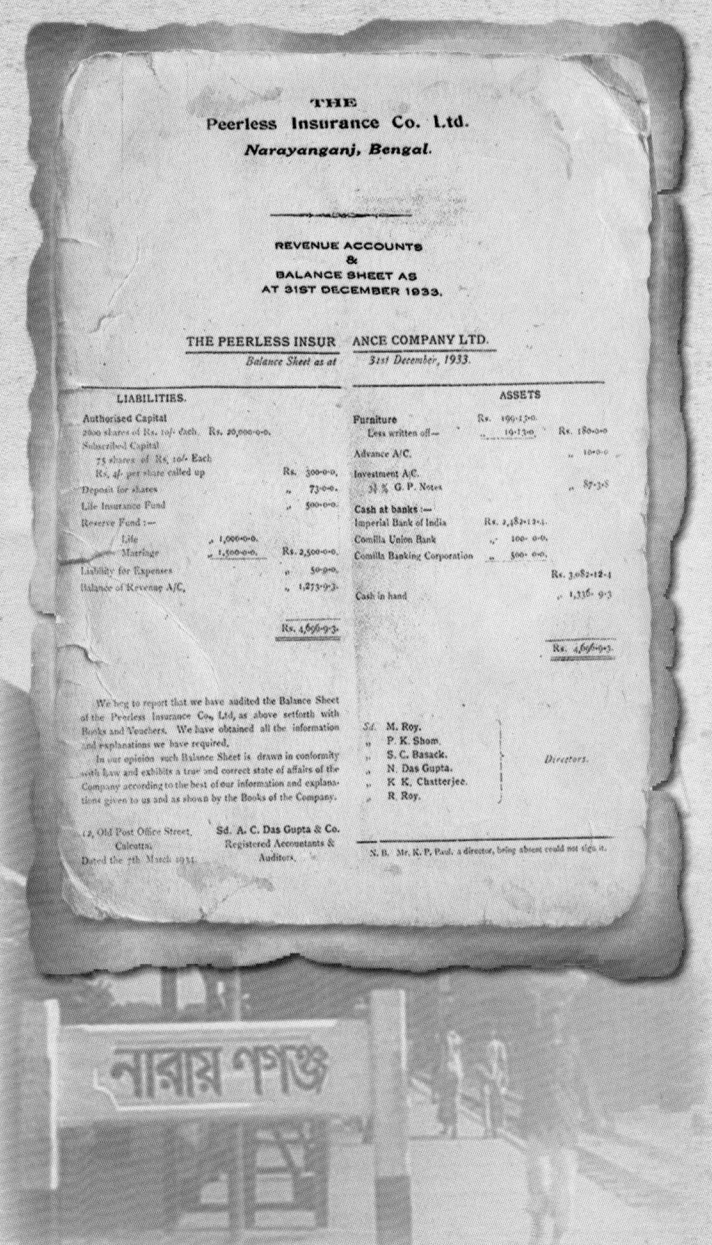

The first balance sheet, along with a view of Narayanganj in Bangladesh where the company began

Shri B.K. Roy – The Architect of Today's Peerless

Shri B.K. Roy at a meeting in his office in Kolkata

Shri B.K. Roy delivering a speech as the conference president at the opening of a branch of a nationalized bank in Kolkata (early 1980s)

Shri B.K. Roy and Shri S.K. Roy attending a meeting at the Peerless Bhavan in Kolkata (1983)

Shri B.K. Roy visiting the flood-affected areas of Medinipur in West Bengal for relief work (1978)

Shri S.K. Roy at a flood relief campaign held in collaboration with Bharat Sevashram Sangha (1978)

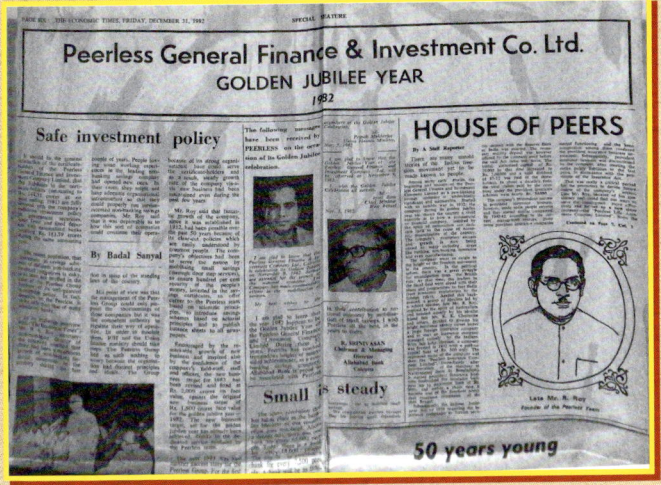

THE ECONOMIC TIMES, FRIDAY, DECEMBER 31, 1982 SPECIAL FEATURE

Peerless General Finance & Investment Co. Ltd.

GOLDEN JUBILEE YEAR

1982

Safe investment policy

By Badal Sanyal

HOUSE OF PEERS

By A Staff Reporter

Late Mr. R. Roy
Founder of the Peerless Team

Small is steady

50 years young

An advertisement of the Peerless Golden Jubilee Celebrations (1982)

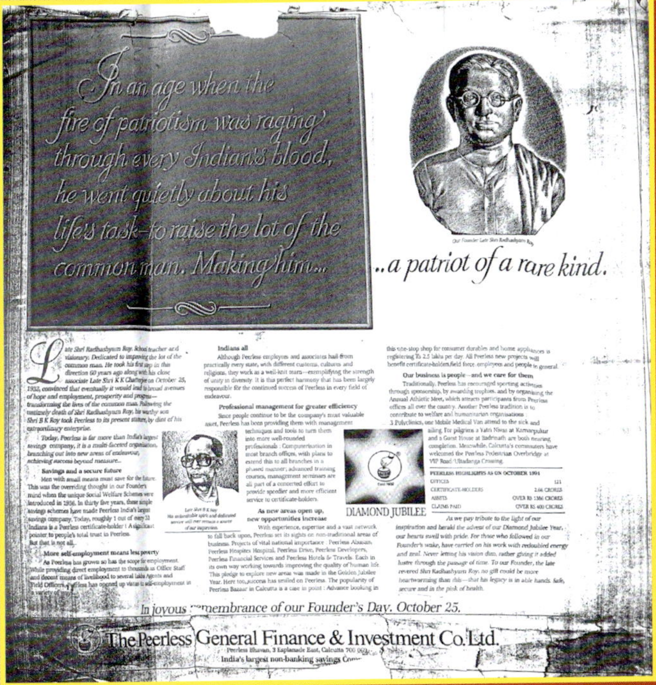

In an age when the fire of patriotism was raging through every Indian's blood, he went quietly about his life's task—to raise the lot of the common man. Making him...

..a patriot of a rare kind.

Our Founder Late Shri Radhashyam Roy

Late Shri Radhashyam Roy. School teacher and visionary. Dedicated to improving the lot of the common man. He took his first step in this direction 60 years ago along with his close associate Late Shri K K Chatterjee on October 25, 1932, convinced that eventually it would lead to broad avenues of hope and employment, prosperity and progress—transforming the lives of the common man. Following the untimely death of Shri Radhashyam Roy, his worthy son Shri B K Roy took Peerless to its present stature, by dint of his extraordinary enterprise.

Today, Peerless is far more than India's largest savings company, it is a multi-faceted organisation, branching out into new areas of endeavour, achieving success beyond measure...

Savings and a secure future

Men with small means must save for the future. This was the overriding thought in our Founder's mind when the unique Social Welfare Schemes were introduced in 1956. In thirty five years, these simple savings schemes have made Peerless India's largest savings company. Today, roughly 1 out of every 33 Indians is a Peerless certificate-holder ! A significant pointer to people's total trust in Peerless. But that is not all...

More self-employment means less poverty

As Peerless has grown so has the scope for employment. While providing direct employment to thousands as Office Staff and decent means of livelihood to several lakhs Agents and Field Officers, Peerless has opened up vistas to self-employment in a variety of ways...

Late Shri B K Roy
His unforgettable spirit and dedicated service will ever remain a source of our inspiration.

Indians all

Although Peerless employees and associates hail from practically every state, with different customs, cultures and religions, they work as a well-knit team—exemplifying the strength of unity in diversity. It is this perfect harmony that has been largely responsible for the continued success of Peerless in every field of endeavour.

Professional management for greater efficiency

Since people continue to be the company's most valuable asset, Peerless has been providing them with management techniques and tools to turn them into more well-rounded professionals : Computerisation in most branch offices, with plans to extend this to all branches in a phased manner; advanced training courses, management seminars are all part of a concerted effort to provide speedier and more efficient service to certificate-holders.

As new areas open up, new opportunities increase

With experience, expertise and a vast network to fall back upon, Peerless set its sights on non-traditional areas of business. Projects of vital national importance : Peerless Abasan, Peerless Hospitex Hospital, Peerless Drive, Peerless Developers, Peerless Financial Services and Peerless Hotels & Travels. Each in its own way working towards improving the quality of human life. This pledge to explore new areas was made in the Golden Jubilee Year. Here too, success has smiled on Peerless. The popularity of Peerless Bazaar in Calcutta is a case in point : Advance booking in this one-stop shop for consumer durables and home appliances is registering Rs 2.5 lakhs per day. All Peerless new projects will benefit certificate-holders, field force, employees and people in general.

Our business is people—and we care for them

Traditionally, Peerless has encouraged sporting activities through sponsorship, by awarding trophies, and by organising the Annual Athletic Meet, which attracts participants from Peerless offices all over the country. Another Peerless tradition is to contribute to welfare and humanitarian organisations : 3 Polyclinics, one Mobile Medical Van attend to the sick and ailing. For pilgrims a Yatri Niwas at Kamarpukur and a Guest House at Badrinath are both nearing completion. Meanwhile, Calcutta's commuters have welcomed the Peerless Pedestrian Overbridge at VIP Road/Ultadanga Crossing.

DIAMOND JUBILEE

PEERLESS HIGHLIGHTS AS ON OCTOBER 1991	
OFFICES	121
CERTIFICATE-HOLDERS	2.66 CRORES
ASSETS	OVER RS 1386 CRORES
CLAIMS PAID	OVER RS 400 CRORES

As we pay tribute to the light of our inspiration and herald the advent of our Diamond Jubilee Year, our hearts swell with pride. For those who followed in our Founder's wake, have carried on his work with redoubled energy and zeal. Never letting his vision dim, rather giving it added lustre through the passage of time. To our Founder, the late revered Shri Radhashyam Roy, no gift could be more heartwarming than this—that his legacy is in able hands. Safe, secure and in the pink of health.

In joyous remembrance of our Founder's Day. October 25.

The Peerless General Finance & Investment Co. Ltd.
Peerless Bhavan, 3 Esplanade East, Calcutta 700 069
India's largest non-banking savings Com...

An advertisement of the Peerless Diamond Jubilee Celebrations (1992)

Shri S.K. Roy – the Guiding Light for Tomorrow's Peerless

Shri S.K. Roy addressing a seminar gathering
at The Peerless Hotel, Kolkata

Shri Jyoti Basu, the then Chief Minister of West Bengal, at the inauguration of the Peerless Hospital and B.K. Roy Research Centre in Kolkata (1992)

Shri Jyoti Basu, the then Chief Minister of West Bengal, handing over the keys to the first resident of Anupama – a real estate joint venture of the West Bengal Government and Bengal Peerless (1998)

Aaheli, an award-winning Bengali restaurant at the Peerless Hotel, Kolkata

Shri S.K. Roy signs the MoU for Peerless Skill Academy and Ramakrishna Mission with Swami Suviranandaji, General Secretary of the Ramakrishna Order, in the presence of Assistant General Secretaries at Belur Math, Howrah

Shri S.K. Roy delivering a motivational speech at a workshop in The Peerless Inn

Shri S.K. Roy receiving the prestigious **Padma Shri** Award for social service from Her Excellency, the 12th President of India, Smt. Pratibha Patil, at the Rashtrapati Bhavan on 31 March 2009

Shri S.K. Roy with his wife, Smt. Shikha Roy, at the Platinum Jubilee Celebrations of Peerless

Shri Jayanta Roy addressing the audience on the company's 85th Foundation Day (2017)

Smt. Debasree Roy Sarkar addressing the audience at an event organized by Peerless Hotels and Resorts (2023)

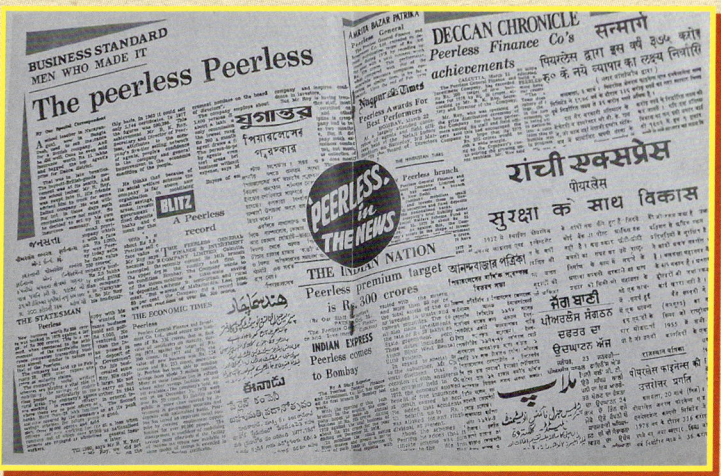

BUSINESS STANDARD
MEN WHO MADE IT
The peerless Peerless

BLITZ
A Peerless record

THE STATESMAN

THE ECONOMIC TIMES

AMRITA BAZAR PATRIKA

DECCAN CHRONICLE
Peerless Finance Co's achievements

Nagpur Times
Peerless Awards For Best Performers

युगान्तर
পিয়ারলেসের পুরস্কার

PEERLESS in THE NEWS

THE INDIAN NATION
Peerless premium target is Rs. 300 crores

INDIAN EXPRESS
Peerless comes to Bombay

सन्मार्ग
पियरलेस द्वारा इस वर्ष ३६५ करोड़ रु० के नये व्यापार का लक्ष्य निर्धारित

रांची एक्सप्रेस
पीयरलेस
सुरक्षा के साथ विकास

आनन्दबाजार पत्रिका

जग बाणी
पीअरलेस संगठन दफ़तर दा उदघाटन अज

ईनाडु

Peerless in the News (1977–78)

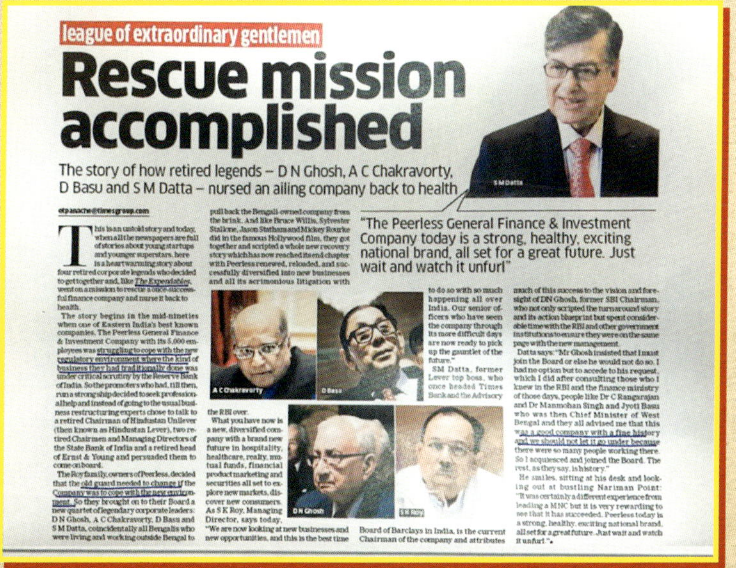

league of extraordinary gentlemen

Rescue mission accomplished

The story of how retired legends – D N Ghosh, A C Chakravorty, D Basu and S M Datta – nursed an ailing company back to health

etpanache@timesgroup.com

This is an untold story and today, when all the newspapers are full of stories about young startups and younger superstars, here is a heartwarming story about four retired corporate legends who decided to get together and, like *The Expendables*, went on a mission to rescue a once-successful finance company and nurse it back to health.

The story begins in the mid-nineties when one of Eastern India's best known companies, The Peerless General Finance & Investment Company with its 5,000 employees was struggling to cope with the new regulatory environment where the kind of business they had traditionally done was under critical scrutiny by the Reserve Bank of India. So the promoters who had, till then, run a strong ship decided to seek professional help and instead of going to the usual business restructuring experts chose to talk to a retired Chairman of Hindustan Unilever (then known as Hindustan Lever), two retired Chairmen and Managing Directors of the State Bank of India and a retired head of Ernst & Young and persuaded them to come on board.

The Roy family, owners of Peerless, decided that the old guard needed to change if the Company was to cope with the new environment. So they brought on to their Board a new quartet of legendary corporate leaders: D N Ghosh, A C Chakravorty, D Basu and S M Datta, coincidentally all Bengalis who were living and working outside Bengal to pull back the Bengali-owned company from the brink. And like Bruce Willis, Sylvester Stallone, Jason Statham and Mickey Rourke did in the famous Hollywood film, they got together and scripted a whole new recovery story which has now reached its end chapter with Peerless renewed, reloaded, and successfully diversified into new businesses and all its acrimonious litigation with the RBI over.

"The Peerless General Finance & Investment Company today is a strong, healthy, exciting national brand, all set for a great future. Just wait and watch it unfurl"

S M Datta

A C Chakravorty

D Basu

D N Ghosh

S K Roy

What you have now is a new, diversified company with a brand new future in hospitality, healthcare, realty, mutual funds, financial product marketing and securities all set to explore new markets, discover new consumers. As S K Roy, Managing Director, says today, "We are now looking at new businesses and new opportunities, and this is the best time to do so with so much happening all over India. Our senior officers who have seen the company through its more difficult days are now ready to pick up the gauntlet of the future."

SM Datta, former Lever top boss, who once headed Times Bank and the Advisory Board of Barclays in India, is the current Chairman of the company and attributes much of this success to the vision and foresight of DN Ghosh, former SBI Chairman, who not only scripted the turnaround story and its action blueprint but spent considerable time with the RBI and other government institutions to ensure they were on the same page with the new management.

Datta says: "Mr Ghosh insisted that I must join the Board or else he would not do so. I had no option but to accede to his request, which I did after consulting those who I knew in the RBI and the finance ministry of those days, people like Dr C Rangarajan and Dr Manmohan Singh and Jyoti Basu who was then Chief Minister of West Bengal and they all advised me that this was a good company with a fine history and we should not let it go under because there were so many people working there. So I acquiesced and joined the Board. The rest, as they say, is history."

He smiles, sitting at his desk and looking out at bustling Nariman Point: "It was certainly a different experience from leading a MNC but it is very rewarding to see that it has succeeded. Peerless today is a strong, healthy, exciting national brand, all set for a great future. Just wait and watch it unfurl."•

A newspaper article on the turnaround story (1996–2015) of Peerless

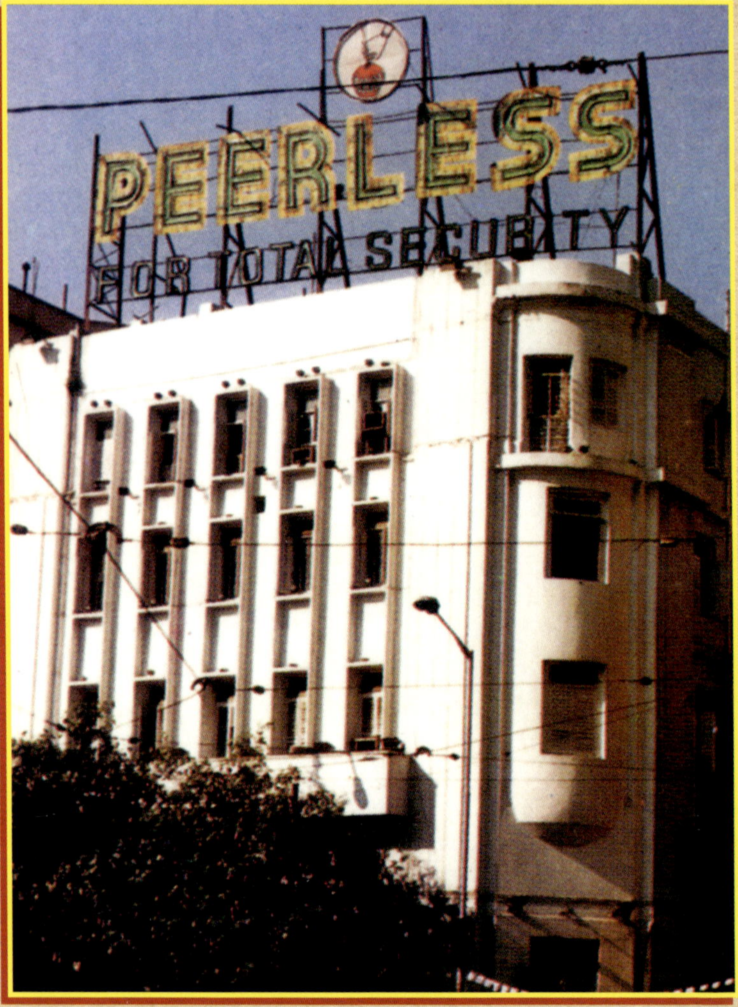

The Peerless Bhavan in Kolkata

The evolution of the Peerless logo since 1932

para-banking sector to malpractice and of the ordinary investor to fraud. Prize chits, said Justice Reddy, had become 'a pan-Indian epidemic'. The total number of people victimized by these projects was considerable, and the injury to the community was substantial. He approved of the intention of the Banning Act, which, he believed, sought to counteract 'the glitter of glamorous prizes, the lure of big money for small.' Such schemes were 'apt to entice the credulous and uncautious.'

This led to his final point, which was a recommendation, not a ruling.

The RBI studied the judgement and rightly set out some much more specific rules, which took full cognizance of the Supreme Court's guidance, the existence of RNBCs and the realities of financial practice on the ground.

Issued on 15 May 1987, and known as the Residuary Non-Banking (Reserve Bank) Directions 1987, the new rules laid down a definition of an RNBC as 'a company, which receives any deposit under any scheme or arrangement by whatever name called, in one lump sum or instalments by way of contributions or subscriptions or by sale of the unit certificates or other instruments, or in any other manner' and which did not conform to the previous definition of a NBFC as laid down in the 1977 Directions. This definition could apply to all the 'mushroom companies'.

Finally, the picture became clear. The Supreme Court judgement and the withdrawal of the reputed conglomerate left P.C. Sen as Chairman and MD, with an open road ahead of him. He had big plans because he knew the company had to outgrow its existing model of taking millions of small deposits. His background was in hard engineering and his vision was a move into manufacturing, retail and beyond. And he had twenty percent of the Peerless net-owned fund with which to do it.

7

New Protocols, New Experiments
(1987–1996)

The new 'road map' for Peerless had four main elements, which were designed in combination to deliver a more secure future under the headings of efficiency, public image, investment and diversification.

P.C. Sen intended to continue with the computerization of the business, fully realizing the way it aided expansion and cut costs. He also made it his policy to open more branch offices, which would cut down journey time for agents in more remote areas. Easier visits to offices meant more time selling policies and less time travelling; more frequent visits to offices meant that agents were more likely to deliver the full value of the original deposits. He also converted the commission payment system into a regular monthly cash flow, giving agents the feel of salaried work, and hence greater security. All these measures would also help to build up the sales force, which was necessary to increase the flow of funds into the company.

He was also acutely conscious, as an outsider, that after the debacle of Ponzi schemes, the informal, 'shadow banking' sector had acquired an adverse image problem. Under the circumstances, he felt it was absolutely necessary to boost the company's reputation in both public and official spheres. 'What we had to do was to make Peerless a respectable household name' he told an audience in early 1996.[1]

To do this, he pursued a multilevel strategy. The top level was to lend money to state governments.

> The moment we lent money to state governments, we became respectable. And what happened is, when one goes to places like Assam and Andhra Pradesh, people generally say, 'Look, you collect money from here and take it to West Bengal.' The agents can say, 'Now, we take money and give it to the government.' So immediately the collection outside West Bengal shot up. The day I left Peerless, there were thirteen state governments

whom we had lent money. This helped the agents enhance the business quicker. He did not have to say Peerless, Peerless, Peerless many times. Because the moment he pronounced Peerless, people recognised it.[2]

In claiming this level of strategic planning, however, Sen was, to some degree, rewriting history. The first of Peerless's loans to a state government was not an entirely voluntary affair, and it didn't come early.

It was a tricky moment, but it didn't work out too badly. A.K. Mukhuty recollects, 'The return on that money was 16 percent, but we lost 2 percent on withdrawal.'[3]

On a more popular level, Sen dabbled in sports sponsorship, especially outside Calcutta. Cannily, he also decided to publish affordable editions of questions and answers for Secondary and Higher Secondary examinations, branded with the Peerless name. 'And what happened was that boys of 16 to 18 years said, "Oh! This is Peerless." So, from 16 we started brainwashing of boys into Peerless.'

Catch them young, hit them hard. 'It was very mild brainwashing,' he added.[4] For older, and perhaps poorer people, Sen committed to opening local polyclinics 'where for ₹2 one can consult with a good doctor. We not only gave a free check-up but even free medicines. And the strategy helped us to make Peerless a household name.'

He felt that times, habits and standards were moving on, and quickly. His pitch to the existing management was, 'Look, you will not be able to run this company in future because slowly other players will come in. And one day the Government of India will not let you carry on this type of business.'[5] For him, diversification was an absolute imperative, and he embraced it wholeheartedly.

Under the stewardship of S.K. Roy with P.C. Sen as the chief executive, a very long string of acquisitions followed, across the whole spectrum of industrial and commercial activities. Hotels were a priority. The former Ritz in downtown Calcutta was acquired and renamed the Peerless Inn. Travel and tourism were viewed as expanding fields; the sector could earn valuable foreign exchange too. Healthcare was also a key target area. B.K. Roy

New Protocols, New Experiments

had always wanted to build a hospital, and in 1992, the Peerless Hospitex Hospital was launched as a joint venture with a French company. Housing was another potentially profitable area, which overlapped well with the Peerless philosophy of community engagement, and Peerless Developers was set up with the intention of building flats for middle- and lower-income groups.

There were also ventures into oil exploration, liquor distilling, tea, electric autorickshaws and budget computers, and dreams of a retail chain to be titled Peerless Bazaar.

The effect on the balance sheet was rapid and dramatic. The company's worth shot up from ₹600 crore to ₹4500 crore in four years. Between 1987 and 1991, the number of branch offices rose from 99 to 121, and the total number of certificate holders increased from 194,00,000 to 266,00,000. In 1990, S.K. Roy became the joint managing director.

But the regulatory problems had not gone away. P.C. Sen was perfectly correct in sensing that the government had continuing concerns about para-banking. And soon enough, Peerless was embroiled again in a difficult situation with the RBI.

The Challenge – Part III (1987–1996)

Regulatory and Compliance Issues

The RBI Directions of 1987 represented a landmark in disciplining the informal financial sector, and there were soon distinct signs that the new regulatory regime was beginning to bite. According to the RBI, prior to 1987 there were 747 companies operating as para-banks, running various deposit schemes. By 1990, this number had fallen to 392; the required information for classifying the remaining companies had not been received. Thirty-five companies had reported a negative net worth, meaning their liabilities were more than their reserves; the negative net worth aggregated to ₹3.6 crore. Only 16 companies, including Peerless, had a positive net worth.

The RBI had serious concerns about the viability of the deposit-taking model and the social implications of that model. This concern prompted a move away from legal exactitude into a wider consideration of all the social and business implications of the small savings business.

Peerless, as the largest operator in the sector, naturally came within their sights. A number of issues and three separate legal actions were all rolled together, leading to a final set of rulings in 1996. And after the vindication of 1987, this time the current was against the company.

This long sequence began in 1988, when another Calcutta-based savings company brought an action against the RBI, questioning the validity of the 1987 Directions, and in particular Paragraphs 6 and 12, which, taken together, it claimed, had rendered its business unviable. Paragraph 6 laid down that RNBCs must lodge one hundred percent of the monies they collected in banks and secure funds, with the implication that they should not use any of those monies to fund the running of their businesses. Paragraph 12 required all RNBCs to treat the deposits they received as liabilities in their accounts, and required them to invest the aggregate amounts of their liabilities. Paragraph 12 thus provided a working definition of what amounts a company should keep invested under Paragraph 6.

While the proceeding was on, a single judge granted an interim order on 7 October 1988, and the RBI duly appealed. The Division Bench of the Calcutta High Court then heard the appeal, during which Peerless became impleaded as a party-respondent, after a demand by the Court to see its account books. On 23 March 1990, the Bench held that the RBI was empowered, under Sections 45J and 45K of the 1934 Act, to issue directions to RNBCs in the interest of depositors. However, 'to the extent that such directions were found to be prohibitory or unworkable and as such unreasonable', any similar regulations would be beyond the powers of the RBI to make. This instruction to rewrite the rules was effectively a win for that Calcutta-based savings company and Peerless.

The RBI appealed to the Supreme Court. Peerless was again represented by Somnath Chatterjee, who contended that the 1987 Directions were ultra vires the powers conferred on the RBI by Sections 45J–K of the 1934 Act, as none of those sections authorized the bank to frame any directions prescribing the manner of investment of deposits received or the method of accountancy to be followed or how its accounts were to be drawn up.

Peerless also maintained that the interest of its depositors had not been impaired in any manner by the method of accountancy that it and all similar companies used, namely, 'appropriation of a part of the subscription to the profit and loss account and meeting the working capital requirements out of the same.'

However, eventually on 30 January 1992, in a judgement that became known as Peerless II, Justices N.M. Kasliwal and K. Ramaswamy upheld the validity of the 1987 Directions and reversed the judgement of the Division Bench.[6]

Meanwhile, further restrictions were introduced within the RNBC sector vis-à-vis reduction of maximum period of deposits, elimination of processing or maintenance charges etc., which was again challenged before the court of law. Judgement was thereafter delivered on 3 May 1995, and the High Court upheld the validity of the notification that limited saving schemes to a maximum of seven years. However, it also held that the notification dated 19 April 1993, under which Paragraph 4-A was introduced in the 1987 Directions, was ultra vires the powers conferred on the bank.

In a familiar pattern, this was an early victory for Peerless. But the matter was again challenged before the Hon'ble Supreme Court. Subsequently, Justice S.C. Agrawal delivered a judgement on 4 January 1996, a decision that became known as Peerless III,[7] thereby declaring, inter-alia, that the RBI was entirely competent to make regulations and the same was binding on the RNBCs.

On a kinder note, he added, 'It cannot be denied that Residuary Non-Banking Companies, like Peerless, play a useful role in the economy by mobilizing savings by tapping that section of the people which the commercial banks are not able to.' But that was all. '[A]t the same time, it cannot be ignored that there should be adequate protection for the funds entrusted to them by depositors and for that purpose, it is necessary that the working of these companies should be closely monitored and supervised. [. . .] The Union government may also consider whether the existing provisions need to be further strengthened to safeguard the interests of the depositors.'

He rejected all the company's arguments, reversed the decisions of the High Court, and thus effectively sank the post-1956 Peerless business model.

The statutory regime had been tightened and it had proved unassailable. The business of collecting small savings could still be carried on but without any of the aspects within it that made it as or more profitable than other businesses. As such, there remained little incentive to carry it on long term in the old style with a large sales force motivated by commission. The old model had provided a degree of security for savings companies and perhaps too little security for depositors, thus rendering them vulnerable to abuse. But with the tables so resolutely turned against the RNBCs, the future of small savings schemes seemed bleak.

P.C. Sen was proved right – the government would not, in the long term, allow Peerless to continue unhindered. But the 1996 judgement had wider implications for him too. P.C. Sen had to step down, on a number of counts.

The appointment of P.C. Sen had been an attempt to find continuity. However, the diversification model he followed was not an easy path. But, more seriously, the regulatory rules were tightening at every turn, no matter what Peerless achieved via the courts or in its practices or its account books.

This really mattered, because the next round in the regulatory battle saw Peerless being forced to recalculate its liabilities on the strict lines laid down in the modified 1987 Directions, and the black hole in the balance sheet that was revealed was potentially fatal for the company. It would also prove difficult to remedy the shortfall because the profits that the old model generated were to be unavailable in future.

Another crisis was just beginning.

8

The Turnaround

(1996–2006)

At the start of 1996, Peerless entered a new realm of uncertainty. With the company's chief executive forced to stand down, and its principal line of business condemned in the courts as illegal – unfair to depositors – where exactly lay the road ahead?

The company did not seem to be in immediate financial danger, sitting as it was on an asset base of ₹4,500 crore, which looked healthy enough. But close supervision from the RBI was about to force an exercise in retrospective accountancy, and what was revealed would soon be a matter of major concern. If all the monies that had been carried across to the profit and loss account were reclassified as full liabilities, in line with the RBI's 1987 Directions, the company's position would be completely changed. In other words, if everything that Peerless was due to pay out had to be kept on deposit or in investments, the company would suddenly have to find ₹771 crore from somewhere.

This figure represented a total of all the money that had been written out of depositors' accounts and used for the payment of commissions and charges. This money had therefore already been spent. The necessity to replace these sums in cash was one of the principal objectives of the next seven or so years. Fortunately for Peerless, its cooperative attitude, coupled with its good record of financial management and its consistent payment of endowment sums on maturity meant that the RBI, led by Governor C. Rangarajan, maintained a lenient stance, and gave the company sufficient time to remedy whatever problems there might be in the balance sheet.

That was the good news – a period of grace was extended to the company. The bad news, however, was that the expansion strategy had simply not delivered enough cash flow to the company. The loan portfolio and many of the subsidiary enterprises had underperformed, leaving the company very short of income at a time when it needed to be making profits to plug the hole in the accounts.

The Turnaround

The story of the next ten years revolves around four priorities; the drive towards positive net worth, the redirection of the company's activities, the reassessment of its subsidiary enterprises, and the rebuilding of its administrative structure.

As the dust settled after the Supreme Court's rulings in January 1996, S.K. Roy found himself in a not dissimilar position from where he had been nine years before. But this time the situation was far more serious.

In January 1987, Peerless had just won an important victory. It had essentially been told that its business was legal and that it could carry on doing what it had been doing. Having ridden out a brief, rocky corporate partnership over the previous year, Peerless had a fresh, energetic executive in place, and a well-furnished war chest to spend.

By contrast, in January 1996, the company had just been told that several aspects of its operations were not in conformity with the law, and it had lost that same executive. Furthermore, while many aspects of the company's financial position seemed favourable, there were a number of unfortunate and unforeseen problems that would have to be surmounted.

The most positive difference in 1996 was that S.K. Roy had the scope to avoid repeating the mistakes of the mid-1980s. This time he did not go looking for investors or a corporate partner who might turn hostile; Instead he resolved to retain control of the company himself and to professionalize the management in a way he had not been able to do on the previous occasion. In this enterprise, he proved extraordinarily successful. This time, he found the right man, a man who understood the problems of corporate and banking finance in India. That man was Dhruba Narayan Ghosh (D.N. Ghosh), and, fortunately, he was also a man of outstanding integrity, who could balance shrewd judgement with a sense of real compassion.

His task, which required him to mobilize all his skills and experience, was to turn around the largest RNBC in India, and to do it as quickly as possible while keeping the company on the right side of the RBI.

Thus began the third pivotal relationship in the history of Peerless after the first between

The Turnaround

Radhashyam Roy and K.K. Chatterjee and the second between B.K. Roy and M.R. Mukherjee – between S.K. Roy and D.N. Ghosh.

With the adverse Supreme Court judgement delivered, and P.C. Sen gone, PGFI was forced to confront two major questions: what kind of profitable business could the company transact, and under whose leadership?

Regarding the first of these questions, the prospect of simply continuing with the deposit-taking model and finding a way to run it more efficiently, while keeping in line with the amended 1987 Directions (plus the subsequent judgements), promised to be a demanding, if not impossible, task. It might have been achievable if the company had been in rude financial health, but it was not.

It soon became uncomfortably clear that, despite all the surface-level activity, the growth of the previous years had an illusory element to it. The company had actually saddled itself with a collection of underperforming assets, including unrecoverable loans and a string of failing subsidiary businesses. This placed a host of uncomfortable decisions before the company, for which strong leadership and vision would be required.

But there was an equally challenging problem lurking within the company's long-term balance sheet, which the litigation against the RBI had highlighted – the issue of the actuarial accounting system. Peerless had been functioning perfectly well with this system in place, and the RBI had been slow to criticize it. But now, after the verdict in 1996, the Reserve Bank's Governor, C. Rangarajan, was taking a much closer interest in all RNBCs. Ultimately, it was this interest that brought D.N. Ghosh to Peerless.

In early 1996 the RBI wanted to find a safe pair of hands to run Peerless, while S.K. Roy was looking for much the same thing. It was a complicated three-way courtship, but eventually all parties found a suitable match.

Roy first approached Ghosh sometime in March or April 1996. Ghosh was aware of the recent developments. 'I had been reading about a protracted battle with the Reserve Bank that

Peerless had lost ultimately in the Supreme Court.' He had also known of previous interest by the RBI and the government of West Bengal as far back as the 1970s, and he was initially cautious about involving himself with an RNBC company, being well versed in the inherent problems of para-banking, and fully aware of the government's increasingly unfavourable view of the sector.

S.K. Roy first caught up with Ghosh in a smart hotel in Calcutta, where the latter was staying while on business for Philips India. Roy offered him the chairmanship of the board. Ghosh was impressed seeing Roy as a responsible person, who sincerely believed that 'he was morally bound ... to honour the commitment to the depositors, a trust since the inception of the company, it had never betrayed.'[1] Nevertheless, Ghosh demurred. From his understanding of the company's position, he foresaw too many difficulties, and felt he had insufficient time to devote to a complex new project on such a scale.

But there was a powerful consensus forming that he was the right man for the job. Ultimately, after much persuasion and detailed deliberations,

Ghosh agreed to join hands with Peerless to cope up with the immediate uncertainties.

Ghosh told Roy that he had to step forward and take responsibility. As chairman, he needed to have a willing partner as managing director. He insisted that Roy was the man, but that he needed freedom to bring in other executives as and when they were needed.

All his conditions were accepted, and D.N. Ghosh was installed as non-executive Chairman in August 1996, with S.K. Roy as Managing Director.

The coalition of personal, regional and national interests that brought Ghosh to Peerless, and his punctiliousness in setting up his installation correctly, were both highly beneficial. Each in its way set the tone for the long-term running of the relationship, and both did a great deal to ensure its success.

At this time, the RBI was also taking a close interest in another RNBC based in Karnataka. The Reserve Bank was sufficiently concerned about its practices to prohibit the organization from taking fresh deposits in October 1998. Peerless was spared such stringent measures partly because of its long record of compliance, and partly because of the bona fide efforts of Ghosh.

'Peerless – they [the RBI] could handle because they knew they could ask me. They knew I was the spokesman. So, they tackled Peerless in a way they were not able to tackle others.'[2] But it wasn't straightforward. 'I had to fight the RBI on behalf of Peerless. I said, "Things might be wrong, but don't touch the company, otherwise I won't be able to manage it".'[3] It was a matter of trust. 'That is where the personal element came in – absolutely personal element. They knew I was not taking money or anything.'[4]

There was a decisive degree of personal connection from the start, which cannot be overstated. This was founded on the working relationships between D.N. Ghosh, C. Rangarajan and S.K. Roy, but it went further, as events were to prove. The whole recovery process that Peerless underwent was as strongly marked by interpersonal trust as it was by hard work and good financial management.

Once Ghosh was in place, a new team would be built around him. First, he brought in Sushim Mukul Datta (S.M. Datta), a prize recruit with a long record of success at the elite level of management, notably as Chairman at Hindustan Unilever. S.K. Roy had originally considered S.M. Datta as a replacement for P.C. Sen, but Datta had declined the offer. Now, things looked a little different. Ghosh and Datta were old associates, and when Ghosh had originally been considering the Peerless job, he called Datta to say, 'I have been asked to become chairman of Peerless. I told them I won't join unless you join me.'[5]

The same network that snared Ghosh now proceeded to whip in Datta. He was encouraged to join the board, as Ghosh had been, by none other than the then Chief Minister, Jyoti Basu, another long-standing acquaintance, who told Datta that if he did not join Peerless, the board would lack credibility. S.M. Datta remembers, 'I told Mr Ghosh I will join. The two of us met the RBI Governor Rangarajan, and it was decided that we will have overriding powers on all matters.'[6] Rangarajan told him, 'We want people like you. We want sincere people to guide Peerless.'[7]

Ghosh also wanted to induct Dipankar Basu, ex-State Bank of India chairman, onto the board, but he had to wait for his man. Basu had to serve out a cooling-off period after standing down from a state-run enterprise, and he was not able to join until 1997.

Finally, Ghosh felt he needed help in a key area – auditing. To do this he called on Amal Chandra Chakrabortti (A.C. Chakrabortti), an experienced accountant who had been prominent at major firms including S R Batliboi and Co and Ernst and Young.

With these three heavyweights, D.N. Ghosh then took on the complex task of reshaping the Peerless Group, with S.M. Datta concentrating on its multiple subsidiary enterprises, Dipankar Basu handling its investments, and A.C. Chakrabortti leading the audit sub-committee.

There was plenty for all of them to do, but the most important relationship within Peerless remained between Ghosh and S.K. Roy. If their liaison had not worked well, the whole situation, both inside and outside the boardroom, could have been very different, and quite possibly the company would have struggled to survive, let alone flourish. Ghosh was no autocrat, but he had a highly immersive way of working, familiarizing himself with fine details, while never losing sight of the bigger picture. Roy gave him the space to work, and constant support.

Ghosh is quick to praise his colleague both professionally and personally. 'S.K. Roy never interfered or questioned decisions. But I also never took decisions without consulting him. Giving due regard to a majority shareholder is not just courtesy, his position demands that.' Ghosh always felt they were on the same side, even when dealing with the legacy of unwise decisions, or questionable practices. 'None of these things were S.K. Roy's fault.'[8] Such constructive attitudes and perceptions undoubtedly helped the two to work in tandem, and Ghosh is genuinely warm about Roy, both in print and in private conversation. 'The relationship that we built up over those turbulent years continues today and I cherish it.'[9]

The new team needed to act quickly. The company posted an enormous net loss of ₹42 crore 22 lakh for the year 1995–96, as compared to a comfortable net profit of ₹9 crore 15 lakh for the previous year. The bubble had burst on the trading account, and with the write-back losses of ₹771 crore, the company was now losing money on its current account while carrying a massive capital deficit.

The final piece of bad news was that the RBI's new regime had more to it than a recalculation of liabilities and quarterly inspections. Following the recommendations of the Shah Committee (1992), in January 1997, the Reserve Bank of India fittingly issued instructions that all NBFCs and RNBCs had to obtain a certificate of registration by January 2003. One of the qualifications was having a positive net worth of at least ₹25 lakh.

The company then submitted its application on 8 July 1997 for registration under Section 451A of the RBI Act 1934 to carry on the business of a non-banking financial institution. The conditions allowed Peerless a window of six years to comply, which might have seemed generous, but rather less so in the light of the extent of the company's shortfall in income. This shortfall then became critical, when another huge hole in the balance sheet appeared, 'because of non-provision for bad, doubtful and non-performing assets. This, along with deferred liability, created overnight, at the end of March 1997, an accumulated deficit of ₹1,396 crore.'[10] Positive net worth seemed a very long way off, and the clock was ticking.

This was something of a perfect storm in corporate terms. Ghosh was bewildered. 'It was a puzzle to me how a company with a full-time professional executive as its Chairman for several years could have gotten itself into such a mess.'[11]

His response was not only to recruit his specialist team, but to call for expert analysis too. He turned to 'a few competent and trusted analysts from ICRA.'[12] ICRA (or IICRA – Investment Information and Credit Rating Agency of India Limited – at the time) was an independent investment analysis company that Ghosh himself had helped to set up. Creating it was a saga in itself, but it proved its usefulness to its creator when needed.

'We had to initiate steps immediately and simultaneously to increase income, reduce costs and ensure recovery from non-performing assets.'[13] This is a neat summary, but the task fell under at least seven main headings: liabilities, deposits, expenses/costs, return on investments, subsidiary companies, staffing levels and labour relations. And several of these categories were interlinked in complex ways. For instance, collecting more deposits was desirable to ease the cash flow, but this would be hard to accomplish without either raising commission rates, which would adversely affect costs, or raising staffing levels, which would have much the same effect. But reducing costs by either redundancy or revising commission rates could have a serious negative impact on the whole group. Finally, under the 1987 Directions as amended, only a tiny fraction of the first year's cash collection could be used to offset running costs.

Generating cash was a priority, and successful subsidiary enterprises were one potential source, but only within the boundaries of the twenty percent 'discretionary quota' that the RBI allowed to RNBCs, and success was not guaranteed in any single case. Shrewd investment was really the key to survival, while ensuring that maturity payments could still be adequately provided for.

The one piece of good news was that the RBI relaxed the limit of ₹10 that could be charged in any one year as a processing charge. Ghosh persuaded Rangarajan to allow RNBCs to charge a one-time non-refundable service charge of ₹80 per annual deposit of ₹500 or less, on a pro-rata basis. This was gratefully acknowledged by the Board in its Report dated 30 September 1996, which acted as both a summary and a kind of watershed moment.

The Board recognizes the implications of the new Directions on the accounting policies of the Company, namely, disclosure of true liability to the depositors and discontinuance of recognizing income out of the capital portion of the deposit accepted. The disallowed portion of the service charges collected since 1st April 1992, together with the residual amount of liability unprovided as on 31st March 1992, aggregated ₹77 crore 22 lakh. The same amount has been credited to the Social Welfare Scheme Fund during the year, thus reflecting the estimated true and fair liability to the respective deposit holders. The Company has treated this sum as Deferred Obligation to be provided in a phased manner on or before the maturity of corresponding deposits.[14]

The Turnaround

Reality – in all its true and fair aspects – had been accepted. From then on, 'Deferred Obligations' was the key concept within the recovery, and it became the driving force to keep the company alive. Failure to keep up would mean the end.

Controlling costs was absolutely vital, especially because the long-term use of the actuarial accounting system had fostered a casual attitude towards expenditure and cost control within the company. Ghosh was eloquent on the subject of taking deposits and treating them in this manner. 'It is free money, unearned money. You are showing a profit right from the beginning. You have money you can play about with. This was the lifeblood of any RNBC at that time. Why did everyone in Peerless think this was the correct thing to do? It was not dishonesty. They were saying: "I am taking a 7-year deposit, I will pay it in 7 years. When that amount becomes due, I will raise that amount." So, it is a question of raising higher and higher deposits. But the more you raise deposits, the more your liabilities increase.'[15]

In a wider view, this is a precise summary of the temptation laid before all the unscrupulous operators in this field. Ghosh was adamant that this was not the Peerless way. 'They didn't default on anything, and didn't follow any nefarious practices.'[16]

The great temptation, in this context, was ignoring how easy it was to underplay the importance of discipline in cost control. Deposit-taking companies could successfully throw overboard the concept of operating margin. What was critical for gauging viability was not the level of the operating margin, but the continuous inflow of deposits, no matter what the transaction cost was, so long as new depositors could be brought into the net and so long as the regulators chose to look the other way.'[17]

In the case of Peerless, the previous management spent money like water, but it was flowing in like a river at the time. Even though he respected the 20 percent discretionary quota ceiling, he still had enough cash to build a whole network of affiliates. Ghosh was scathing about this profligacy. 'Counterfactually, Peerless made no profit from that 20 percent. In fact, if they had put it in government securities, they would have made more money.'[18]

But now all he and his team could do was to pick up the pieces. They found cases of indiscriminate lending, inadequate supervision of subsidiaries and levels of commission on collection that were disproportionately high. All these were evidence of a carefree cash-rich style of management.

'Much to my horror I discovered that Peerless had spawned twenty-seven subsidiaries – hospital, IT, shipping, real estate . . . you name it,' Ghosh said.[19] Not only were many of them not bringing money in, some were sucking it out. 'When I came on the scene, I found that most of these [subsidiaries] were money guzzlers and not money earners.' Opportunities had been lost. 'If Peerless had given adequate attention to the management of these companies and returns from these investments, it could have emerged as one of the biggest industrial houses in West Bengal.'[20]

The subsidiaries were pruned, with S.M. Datta in charge. Non-performing assets were either written off or sold as they were. It wasn't always easy, remembers Datta. 'There was resistance from within [the management] as each of the subsidiaries was like a child to them. My job was to convince them that we were doing the right thing. The RBI sword was always hanging there. (But) there were not too many hard battles. Roy and his deputy, Bhargab Lahiri, were keen to collaborate with us.'[21]

Bimal Jalan took over from C. Rangarajan as Governor of the RBI in November 1997, and he thought an obvious candidate for a sell-off was the Peerless Hospitex Hospital. It had struggled to turn a profit and had not thrived under the previous management. But D.N. Ghosh was convinced that it could pull through and he fought, successfully, to keep it.

The burden on the company's finances was slowly lifted. What remained was leaner, fitter and more clearly related to the company's core competencies. It was this period that first saw the rational contraction of Peerless's activities into the shape it retains today, with a central interest in financial services, healthcare, hospitality and housing.

Next came a review of the company's investments, including its large and fairly chaotic loan portfolio. 'The loan assets were mostly non-performing and the chances of recovery looked grim. These borrowers had, almost without exception, approached Peerless after having exhausted all other sources of raising money. It was a mystery to me then, and continues to be so now, why these loans were so readily granted; any organization with a modicum of business sense would have kept out of it. These loan assets gave little steady income and, in many cases, the principal amounts were at risk.'[22]

Those who saw P.C. Sen in action recall that he was generous and easy with funding. To ask was to receive, but there was rarely much in the way of follow-up. That job now fell to Dipankar Basu, whose banking expertise was as invaluable to Peerless in this area as S.M. Datta's corporate experience was in the restructuring of its subsidiaries. Here, though, the eventual aim was not just recovery and disinvestment, but redeployment at better rates of return.

In this he proved very successful, aided by the general fall in interest rates over the period. 'The drop in interest rates in early 2000 was an opportunity to make money by trading bonds as their prices rose; the Peerless Treasury made money with both hands.'[23]

As importantly, bad debts had to be tidied up, by whatever means necessary. The Directors' Report of 16 November 1998 listed these as 'regular follow-ups, personal interaction, moral persuasion and relentless pressure' as well as a final resort to legal action, where unavoidable. But 'recognising the inordinate delay in court proceedings, the Company in many cases was successful in arriving at out-of-court settlements with upfront payments, with some reasonable concessions. Such recoveries have not only reduced the levels of NPAs [Non-Performing Assets], with consequential reduction in the provisioning requirements, but also have augmented income through investments made out of such receipts.'

Some of those receipts were from official bodies. 'For loans to some state governments proving difficult to recover, we did not hesitate to go to the extent of taking them to court. The two key persons who did a remarkable job in this area were Bhargab Lahiri and Patit Paban Ray,'[24] remembered D.N. Ghosh. This was all a double bonus – less money out, more money in. The cutting away of dead wood and the redeployment of funds into active trading was an absolutely vital element of the whole turnaround strategy. The reinvestment was the work of a dedicated team led by Dipankar Basu, who 'knew active trading'[25] ably backed up by A.K. Mukhuty.

'The RBI took back the 20 percent discretionary quota, and told us to put everything into securities. This was during the time of Mr Vajpayee.[26] At that point, 14 percent government securities came down to 4.75 percent, and in two years of trading we made around ₹600 crore. So out of 1,200 crore, we made 600 crore – thanks to Mr Vajpayee.'[27]

This was, of course, very beneficial in terms of cash flow, but there were other considerations. Moving funds around helped compliance with the new RBI norms regarding investments. 'The investment in approved securities was only 56 percent as against the statutory requirement of 80 percent.'[28] This figure was gradually approached. Meanwhile the tangle of issues surrounding the costs of collections and staffing levels remained to be addressed. Along with income and expenditure, operating margin could not be ignored.

First consideration was the field force and its incentive structure.

D.N. Ghosh wrote, 'When I joined in August 1996, I found that the net margin was ₹71 crore, while collection-related and operational expenses were much higher, at ₹150 crore. The cost of collection of deposits during 1995–96 was at an extraordinary level of 22 percent.'[29]

The shortfall mainly consisted of agents' commission, which had always been set at a high level to incentivize sales activity. Now, in a more cost-conscious era of management, the commission levels seemed disproportionate, and steps had to be taken to streamline the system. One major problem was the pyramid structure of the field force, with a hierarchy of agents, supervisors and so forth, all of whom shared commission between them, with the senior figures taking a greater overall share for themselves.

The structure had built up to as many as eighteen tiers. If this number could be rationalized, the amount of overall commission might be commensurately reduced as well. This made economic sense, but a reduction in incentives risked potential demoralization on the ground, leading to a fall in the uptake of new certificates. Fewer agents selling fewer policies was a real possibility, and would be the reverse of the original intention.

This is where S.K. Roy's knowledge of the sales force and the details of Peerless's business yet again proved crucial.

> We needed, however, to move cautiously in cutting the flab as we were dependent on these top leaders to maintain the inflow of deposits at a certain level – a must to meet the maturity payments. [...] Reorganization of the field force without affecting its efficacy was of paramount importance. Thanks to the excellent rapport that S.K. Roy enjoyed with the field organization at all levels, he was successful, over a period of three years, in reducing the 18-tier structure to a maximum of five, thereby enabling us to bring down the cost of collection to about 5 or 6 percent.[30]

This was a quarter of what it had been and reflected a reduction in average rates of commission from 20 percent in 1995 to 5.7 percent in the year spanning 1999–2000.

But the ride was hardly smooth. 'During this transition period, our collections had been stagnating – at a level of ₹350 to 400 crore.'[31] This was not enough, and the company was still posting yearly losses, at a time when a surplus was an absolute necessity to achieve positive net worth and service the Deferred Obligations on the balance sheet.

The figures were, however, heading the right way. The net loss was ₹30.82 crore for 1996–97, reducing to ₹17.80 crore 1997–98, and then to ₹6.79 crore 1998–99. Even better, collections were rising, totalling ₹639 crore for 2001–02 and ₹901 crore the year after. 'With this inflow of funds, we never faced any problem of liquidity in meeting maturity commitments. That was a great relief.'[32]

Hidden in these figures was a personal triumph for S.K. Roy. Raising new funds was absolutely crucial in attaining viability and qualifying for registration, without which the company's life would be over. But who would willingly take out a seven-year savings plan with a company that was known to have issues with liquidity? The company's published accounts told a sorry tale, and the press carried stories of asset wipe-out. In such a scenario, public confidence could evaporate, killing off the Peerless brand more effectively than any action by the RBI.

In this moment, the energy and charisma of S.K. Roy were put to full use. He personally fronted a nationwide sales drive that raised the record sum of over ₹900 crore in new business. This effort floated the company on a wave of new cash and restored the standing of the Peerless brand. D.N. Ghosh accompanied him through much of the tour, and cheered Roy's achievement.

'During 1997–99, we had to raise cash to meet our commitments. While you are clearing the past, you cannot default on deposits. S.K. Roy was ideal for this task. He knew the depositors, distributors, agents all over India. Peerless was saved from default by raising money,' said Ghosh. There is no doubt in his mind, 'S.K. Roy saved the company.'[33]

But there was still one final obstacle to overcome – the costs of the large permanent staff. Making savings here would be fiercely resisted, but the logic of slimming down the workforce was irresistible.

D.N. Ghosh was convinced that the company could not reach viability with the 'huge office staff' they had to cover. As the company approached the break-even point, Ghosh began to prepare the final area of cost reduction.

'At one AGM, purposely, I saw a man in the audience ask a planted question, "How many people are needed?" I replied, "Four or five hundred, not three and a half thousand." The unions were furious, but I set the ball rolling.'

The unions, understandably, were reluctant to see cuts. 'They said, "You are destroying employment. We must find a way out." I said there is no way out.'[34]

He suggested a redundancy package. The unions refused. 'Their point of view was that Peerless had always been an ideal employer, generating and preserving employment, and that they would oppose any cost reduction strategies. Their advice was that my strategy should be to increase income and rescue the company, leaving the field force and the employees untouched.'[35]

Ghosh then came under personal attack, with public accusations that he was lining his own pocket, that he had somehow benefited from the study he had called for by ICRA. 'It became bitter.'[36] In response, he did two things. He launched a Voluntary Redundancy Scheme (VRS) in August 2000, and he went to Chief Minister Jyoti Basu to tell him that an employee separation scheme had become unavoidable.

'I put it to him, as politely and mildly as one could, that, without his assurance I would not have shouldered this responsibility and we had now reached that critical point where I was at a dead end.' Jyoti Basu asked for a few days to discuss the matter with union leaders. When they met again, Ghosh was adamant that the redundancies had to go through, and that the alternative was the liquidation of the company.

The Chief Minister then convened leaders of both the CITU and the INTUC, plus senior members of the Congress Party, to broker a deal. 'Somebody questioned the figures. Jyoti Basu said, "He has been with me for many, many years, I trust him." That cleared it.'[37]

So, an agreement was reached. Redundancies would be accepted, but with a good package. 'He kept the commitment he had given me when I accepted the assignment.'[38]

Out of 4,298 employees, 2,762 opted for the scheme, which saved the company a massive ₹40 crore a year.

Finally, all the retrenchment, restructuring, disinvestment and cost control showed through in the books. 'The same year, 2000–01, we tasted a net profit of ₹34 crore as against losses in earlier years. Within the next two years, the entire accumulated deficit of ₹1,396 crore was completely wiped out.'[39]

Peerless then attained positive net worth in October 2002. The application for registration was submitted in January 2003, and the certificate was issued on 9 May 2003.

This represented a real triumph for the whole team. The company had been redesigned and refashioned in multiple ways. It was modernized and rationalized, well-funded and fully compliant.

The Turnaround

It had also diversified in a carefully constructed and sustainable way. The two main problems of the company in the early 1990s, according to Dipankar Basu, had been 'unfocused diversification and not having enough professional managers to run the show.'[40] Both issues had now been addressed and remedied.

Another major shift had been the realignment of the company's financial offers. New fixed deposit schemes were introduced in June 1997 for maturity periods of 18, 36 and 60 months. In November 2000, Ghosh had used the annual report to announce, 'Our aim is to emerge as the country's largest doorstep retail distributor of financial products in the private sector and with the lowest servicing cost for our clients. We are committed to re-establish Peerless presence through visibility, awareness, and accessibility and create increased trust and confidence among the common public.'[41] By the summer of 2001, this policy had produced a tie-in with IFFCO-Tokio for developing 'co-products'.

By November 2002, Ghosh was able to announce,

Things have improved significantly over the past six years. From a negative surplus of ₹109 crore in 1995–96, we have posted a surplus of ₹501 crore during 2001–02 . . . We have actually wiped off the massive shortfall in net owned fund which arose in the wake of the honourable Supreme Court judgement in January 1996 . . . This is a saga of turnaround, of which your company can be legitimately proud. It was committed teamwork, with focus on thrust areas and basics of management, that saw us through. Indeed, a very tough and long journey.[42]

By September 2003, the position was even better.

We have overcome the challenges we faced in the wake of the judgement of Supreme Court in January 1996. The accumulated deficit of ₹1,396 crore including the NPAs, as on 31st March 1996, has been completely wiped off . . . At the end of March 2003, capital adequacy ratio (CAR) stood at 14.56 percent as against the minimum norm of 12 percent.' And the company was further compliant. 'The investment portfolio was restructured raising our investments in the categories approved by the Reserve Bank of India. This was raised from 43 percent March 1997 to about 92 percent as on March 2003, as against the requirement of 80 percent.[43]

By August 2004, the last elements of the recovery were in place. 'The company started this year with a positive net worth of ₹230.30 crore and capital adequacy ratio of 14.56 percent and further strengthened its financial position with a CAR of 23.4 percent. The current norm is 12 percent.'[44]

The figures finally looked good. But though the enormous collective effort seemed to have righted whatever wrongs there were in both legal and management senses, Peerless was not to enjoy an untroubled future.

The Challenge – Part IV (1996–2006)

Regulatory and Compliance Issues

Given the viability achieved, official opinion changed with the arrival of a new governor at the RBI. Y. Venugopal Reddy was installed in September 2003, and he took a different view of RNBCs from his two immediate predecessors,

Rangarajan and Jalan, under both of whom he had served as Deputy Governor. The new regime was not supportive enough for the RNBCs. There was a legitimate dislike for the informality of the RNBC world, particularly in the areas of their deposit-taking activities, such as the problems that arose in enforcing compliance with the new 'Know Your Customer' criteria.

He is quite explicit in his memoir, *Advice and Dissent: My Life in Public Service*. 'The [RNBC] business model itself was unviable unless inappropriate banking practices were adopted. We took a decision to tighten the regulation to an extent that the category would cease to exist. We also felt that it was necessary to provide them an opportunity to exit from this model to avoid disruption. Out of five RNBCs, three quickly exited and two were remaining. These two (Peerless and Sahara), however, accounted for over 60 per cent of the total NBFC sector.'[45]

He felt that RNBCs had reached a natural end to any positive role as financial bodies and had become superfluous to the nation's needs. This marked a distinct change of attitude from the RBI towards several aspects of the Supreme Court's rulings. Consistently through the three cases, judges had drawn attention to the interests not just of depositors – which was the RBI's main concern – but also to the interests of employees. Under Rangarajan and Jalan, the RBI had stayed its hand, with the issue of employment carrying due weight. This restraint was now cast aside, and a new focus on financial propriety took centre stage. RNBCs were now living on borrowed time.

Sure enough, in June 2004, *The Economic Times* ran a story headlined, 'RBI Hardens RNBC Investment Norms', which was a report of the annual Policy Statement by Governor Reddy. New restrictions were to be imposed on the para-banking sector. NBFCs were to be stopped from raising deposits from the public, while RNBCs would have to observe stricter guidelines on their investment practices. Reddy announced that despite their 'useful' role in rural areas, para-banks were 'not transparent in lending operations'. Nor was there a good paper trail between agents and depositors, because they tended to operate through field agents, not branches.

The previous requirement on RNBCs had been to invest 80 percent of their deposits in government and approved securities while they were free to invest the other 20 percent where they wished. Now the RBI wanted to raise the requirement to 90 percent by 2005 and all of it by 2006.[46]

Fortunately, for Peerless, the turnaround undertaken since 1996 had equipped it to move beyond the RNBC business, with excellent prospects of creating a whole new identity for the group. By this point, D.N. Ghosh felt he had accomplished what he had set out to do. He felt relieved, like 'a harassed midwife' who had managed 'to save both mother and the child'.[47] In ten years, Peerless had been revamped from top to bottom and made fit to move forward into new areas. The company was more than solvent and completely compliant with all prudential norms and legal requirements.

He fully appreciated the changing environment. In September 2005 he told the AGM:

> The genesis of RNBCs can be traced to the time when the Indian financial market was relatively

unorganised and depositors had limited access to established and reputable savings institutions . . . The mainstay of your company has been low denomination savings products distributed through our vast agents' network.

As you are all aware, the market for financial products has now significantly expanded making inroads in the relatively sheltered markets in which your company has been operating. There has been a phenomenal growth in the number of bank branches in smaller towns and villages. Mutual funds and life insurance are dominant in the market with a variety of innovative financial products. A shift in peoples' preferences for such products is clearly visible. In this perspective, response to recurring deposit schemes, that have been netting the bulk of the company's collections, is gradually becoming lukewarm.[48]

And there were safe hands ready to accept the baton of leadership. He announced his resignation at the AGM on 19 August 2006, saying Dipankar Basu would succeed him as Chairman.

His valedictory speech that day is worth quoting at length. While fully acknowledging the collective effort he had headed, he made a special mention of the Recovery Committee, Subsidiary Review Committee, Investment Committee and Audit Committee. He emphasized that the management of investments had been professionally organized, and that income from investment operations had been one of the main sources of profit for the company. He also noted that 'the turnaround would not have been possible without a fully committed and dedicated team of executive management who rose up to the demands of the grim challenge and the operation with remarkable perseverance and meticulous detail.' He added, '. . . even with an experienced team of directors and an executive management team that showed their determination to pull out and rescue the company from a near disaster situation, all this would not have been possible without the willing cooperation, commitment and loyalty of our employees at all levels.'

He also had wise words of warning for the future.

The Turnaround

The rosy picture of the present is unlikely to repeat itself, year in and year out. As enlightened shareholders, you have to read the warning signals.

First, the structure of regulation for RNBCs has undergone significant changes . . . With effect from 1 April 2006, RBI has prescribed that the entire investment would have to be in fixed income securities, removing thereby the flexibility that your company had been enjoying in the past for exploiting opportunities for investment in different kinds of market instruments, thereby enhancing the return on investment. With persistent representations, we have got reprieve for a year in respect of 5 per cent of the average liability to the depositors as on 31 December 2005 till 31 March 2007.

While we gratefully acknowledge RBI's gesture, we cannot at the same time afford to ignore the signal that is emanating from the regulatory authority; that signal is loud and clear. We would be deluding ourselves if we believe that the RBI would continue with their forbearance for any indefinite length of time, even though it might adversely affect the viability of the existing

RNBC business model.

The shareholders must be prepared to change the current business model and explore the options available for changing the business model in a way that can keep the company viable within the norms laid down by the regulatory authority.

Second, shareholders have to take a critical look at the competitive market conditions in the financial services business and reflect on the continued viability of the RNBC business model that has flourished at the time when market interest rates were regulated and the company could easily tap deposits of long-term duration from relatively underserviced market segments in the rural and semi-urban areas through field agents.

The scene has undergone a sea change now. The rural and semi-urban market is not as unsophisticated as it used to be. Savers there are now aware of the different kinds of financial products that are now on offer in the market; banks, mutual funds, and insurance companies are exploring innovative ways of capturing clients in these markets which we had once taken for granted as our 'captive' customers. Our distribution network is thinning out and it may not be long before we find ourselves critically short of competent field staff to push our financial products in preference to others.[49]

He reassured the shareholders that all these problems were recognized and that plans were in place to tackle them.

Summing up, he said, 'Tomorrow's challenge will be tougher than yesterday's.'[50]

9

Towards a New Model

Despite the cautionary note in mid-2006, the company's strong performance continued.

In September 2007, Dipankar Basu was able to announce that 'The year has ended with profits of ₹184 crore as against ₹117 crore the previous year, reflecting an increase of 57 percent.' The position of the net owned fund had further improved, reaching ₹693 crore, up from ₹534 crore the previous year. 'Capital adequacy ratio remained at a high-level throughout the year, well above the minimum statutory requirement of 12 percent. As on 31 March 2007, the ratio touched 85.77 percent.'[1]

This really was an excellent performance, and reflected how thoroughly the revamp had been on both income and expenditure sides.

But Basu also had a revelation that day. '... The RBI has, in fact, advised the company earlier in the current financial year that the company may explore an alternate business model and migrate to such a model within a period of three years. The company has, of course, represented to Reserve Bank for a longer transition period, as it would be difficult to accomplish the task of identifying a new business model and then transit thereto within a period of three years. Representation is being followed up with Reserve Bank.'[2]

Governor Reddy had finally made the long-threatened move.

All that remained then were choices, good or bad. Peerless could fight the order through the courts, but this held little attraction. It had been tried before and brought only expense and uncertainty. And ultimately, even a win would not be enough when fighting a regulatory body that could simply rewrite any of its own rules if it lost.

Nor, as in 1992, could adjustments be made to the deposit-taking business to try and comply with a new regime. The RNBC model was effectively outlawed, with a short grace period allowed for companies to adjust. So, the best that PGFI could do was to plead for more time. And that is what it did. The original deadline was 2010, but representations succeeded in extending this by one year, to 1 April 2011.

All that then remained was to further restructure the company's activities to accommodate the loss of the savings schemes.

In the event, this did not prove too difficult. There were already plans afoot to reorient the company as a broad-spectrum purveyor of financial services. There was much in the existing infrastructure – branch offices, computer networks, and sales force – that could easily be adapted to selling financial products that were managed by other companies, not to mention the large existing client base. This looked like a promising avenue, and so it proved.

Thus, Basu was also able to announce that 'Peerless Developers Limited (PDL), one of the subsidiaries of your company, was appointed as corporate agent of Max New York Life Insurance Company for distributing its life insurance products.' Furthermore, 'PDL has also recently entered into the corporate agency of IFFCO-Tokio General Insurance Company Limited for distributing some of their products.'[3]

For some time, there had also been talks of setting up a new mutual fund business. Though D.N. Ghosh had been initially cool about the idea, he believed that such a business was better centred in Mumbai than Calcutta. But Basu confided, 'The Company applied for and has also received approval of RBI for distributing Mutual Fund products and steps are under way to commence such distribution . . . Your company intends to enter the mutual fund business and, to this end, an Asset Management Company is being promoted by Peerless Securities Ltd, a subsidiary of your company. An in-principle approval has already been received from Securities and Exchange Board of India [SEBI] in this regard and further steps are afoot towards implementation of this project.'[4]

There was plenty of constructive thinking here, but the ambition went further. Basu also declared that, 'All four subsidiaries are now operating profitably but the aggregate profit from these subsidiaries is still not significant. Your board is, therefore, now exploring the feasibility of scaling up the businesses of these subsidiaries, so that they can, in future, contribute significantly more to the earnings of your company.'[5]

S.K. Roy remained clear-minded and at the forefront. 'It is my dream to ensure that Peerless is India's premier financial supermarket specially tailored to each Indian's needs. Our goodwill and the trust of five crore satisfied customers, thanks to our unblemished record of maturity payments to the tune of nearly ₹20,000 crore, it will go a long way in ensuring this.' And he appreciated the need for flexibility. 'We have now moved beyond distribution of financial products and introduced our own Mutual Fund – the first from the eastern region through our subsidiary, the Peerless Funds Management Company Limited. We aspire to introduce many more financial products, including insurance.'[6]

The ambition and vision for the Peerless Group were thus plentiful through the early years of the transition away from the RNBC business. All that remained was the task of effective implementation. How easily could all this be accomplished?

There were problems in certain areas, and it proved difficult to move far away from the four main subsidiary areas – healthcare, hotels, housing and financial services. And those areas did not offer easy opportunities for expansion.

But the Group remained secure, and because of its sustained profitability, its net worth breached the ₹1,000 crore mark in 2009. A new kind of stability had arrived, with only the shocks, twists and turns of global financial markets to buffet the company, instead of regulatory innovations and legal issues.

The RBI deadline duly passed in spring 2011, and that year S.K. Roy was able to announce, 'In compliance with guidelines from regulatory authorities, Peerless has exited the RNBC business and is now focused on the Financial Products Distribution (FPD) business. We have been successfully engaged in the distribution of Life Insurance, General Insurance and Mutual Fund products of renowned principals . . . We are now offering our Field Agents an opportunity to become employees of one of our Subsidiaries, subject to conditions. We will also leverage their expertise for non-sales related customer support services.'[7] Meanwhile the performance of the subsidiaries and associate companies had been 'satisfactory'.

The unions had one last, despairing attempt at preserving the old model. *The Economic Times* dated 21 September 2012 reported that 'the new plan has failed to give any sense of hope to the dejected employees' union, which is anticipating a job cut. PGFI has some 1,500 employees and many of them had turned redundant after the company completely stopped mobilizing public deposits from April 2011. 'We don't expect the proposed venture to absorb all these people,' said Gautam Chatterjee, general secretary of All India Peerless Employees Union. 'So, our demand for restoration of the deposit-taking business remains firm.'[8]

But there was no reprieve and no revival.

The RNBC business did take some time to tidy up. In 2014, the company made arrangements with United Bank of India to hold investments equivalent to the liabilities to deposit holders in their custody. As Bhargab Lahiri, who had been promoted to deputy managing director in 2010, explains, 'In a letter dated 31 October 2014, the RBI advised the company to put the unpaid/unclaimed amount into Escrow Account. In accordance with a further order of the High Court, Calcutta, newspaper notifications were published in all leading newspapers of India, advising to submit claim from the depositors, for their unclaimed maturity amount, if any. Accordingly, claims are coming and after scrutiny by us, and according to our advice, UBI is dispersing the unclaimed maturity amounts to those depositors.'[9]

The first major change of the post-RNBC era came in 2014 when Dipankar Basu stood down and S.M. Datta became Chairman. Here was more continuity, as he declared his intention to keep 'widening the scope of our financial services capabilities while strengthening our existing interest in hospitality, healthcare and real estate. Among the various capabilities the Peerless Group has developed in the financial services space are asset management, securities, financial products distribution and lending.'[10]

All this was completely in step with both the historic mission of Peerless, and with the forward vision of S.K. Roy, which he set out at length.

The company's continuous focus of staying true to its core values of honesty, integrity and customer satisfaction have to be adhered to with new age connection tools to maintain its glory.

Towards a New Model

Within a tremendously competitive business environment, we are currently engaged in remodelling our business. The remodelled financial products distribution business is the lifeline of the company and has the potential to play a significant role with its new model. Our future is largely dependent on our capability, efficiency and strength of doing this business. The state-of-the-art IT system has been providing all the support needed to resolve grievances, sort out issues and provide the best customer service.

The Peerless Group promises to stand by the people of the country with services that will help them move closer to their dreams. At the same time, we must never forget that Peerless Group believes in giving back to society as much as it takes, continuing to stand by the underprivileged and distressed at the hour of need.[11]

The second major change came in 2016, with the sale of the Mutual Fund business to the Essel Group. Incorporated in 2009, the fund had grown to hold managed assets of ₹970.88 crore.[12]

PGFI was now a tightly focused company, supervising a cluster of long-term successes that the group had built up since the early 1990s.

Finally, in April 2019 the last of the RNBC business was cleared up. As A.K. Mukhuty explains, 'Some amounts, some unclaimed plans are still there, which are not even matured for seven years. There was ₹1,500 crore of unclaimed funds. ₹900 crore was the principal amount, and the balance was the interest accrued on this ₹900 crore. Now we have placed all this with the Investor Education Protection Fund (IEPF). They send us the claims from depositors, to be verified. We then send them back and they make the payments.'[13]

The Challenge – Part V (2006–2023)

Regulatory and Compliance Issues

After the exit of P.C. Sen, Peerless found the third able successor in S.K. Roy. With S.K. Roy's guiding acumen, the company was efficiently operating its RNBC business in accordance with the rules and regulations framed by RBI. Yet again between 2006 and 2011, Peerless withdrew from

RNBC in due course as per the directive of RBI. In 2015, the company also duly complied with RBI in transferring the unclaimed funds to the Escrow Account.

Four years later, in 2019, as advised by RBI, Peerless arranged to transfer the entire unclaimed funds, amounting to more than ₹1,500 crore, kept in the Escrow Account, to the Investor Education Protection Fund (IEPF) under the Ministry of Company Affairs, Government of India. However, IEPF demanded payment of interest on the unclaimed amount. which has been challenged and the matter is now sub judice.

Considering the consistent bona fide actions of Peerless, the RBI awarded the status of Non-Banking Financial Companies – Investment and Credit Company (NBFC-ICC) to Peerless. With RBI's approval to change the status of the company from Residuary RNBC to NBFC-ICC, the new license in 2023 comes as a breath of fresh air with self-regulation as the new watchword. Investment criteria and limits are more liberal, whether in the group entities or externally. The NFBC-ICC model will allow PGFI to invest across a gamut of securities (without restrictions) under the umbrella limits specified by RBI, instead of seeking approvals for individual investments. This will enable the company to optimize returns and explore more opportunities for steady growth. As a Group, Peerless will invest in core consumer facing businesses for holistic progress and advancement.

Over nine decades, the perseverance, grit and character of three generations have been in place. The new leadership has the onus to gift this legacy to the next generation now.

10

The Guiding Light for Future

S.K. Roy (2006–2022)

S.K. Roy's style was very different from that of his father and brother, though no less successful. The Group's asset base has grown substantially under his stewardship. He retained the central direction of policy but preferred to delegate the detailed work to others, and he proved reliably shrewd in his recruitment choices. It was at this moment that some of the company's long-term officials were allowed to step forward and shine, while expert leadership was drafted in from India's corporate management elite.

S.K. Roy knew the Peerless business very well. He had joined the company in 1969, and then worked his way up through the ranks, joining the Board of Directors in 1984, eventually becoming joint Managing Director in 1990. He was thoroughly imbued with the company's philosophy, having worked closely with his elder brother, late into the night and often across weekends, in the Roy family style of keeping no fixed hours.

As he put it himself, 'I had lost my father at the age of 16, and it was my Dada,[1] who was literally my father figure, guiding me, shaping my insights, helping me hone my talents. I started at the lowest rung – as an assistant secretary – that too after spending a year in the organisation as an apprentice.'[2]

D.N. Ghosh adds, 'S.K. Roy's forbearance in witnessing majority of the twenty-seven companies – that he owned – being closed down was exemplary. And then to resurrect himself the way he did would not have been possible unless he had a deep personal and spiritual feeling. It is inconceivable otherwise. Such quiet courage to recover from huge losses was inspirational. His association with the Ramakrishna Order and living a life dedicated to the teachings of the Holy Trio – Sri Ramakrishna, Holy Mother Sri Sarada Devi and Swami Vivekananda – was a blessing upon him. Undoubtedly, the relevance of spiritual quality which was evident in Radhashyam Roy and

B.K. Roy in leading Peerless was also manifested in S.K. Roy's life.'

He was a man of plain and modest tastes. His office contained nothing ostentatious, apart from a few trophies and awards that Peerless had accumulated under his leadership. He was acutely conscious of the legacy he took on from his father and elder brother; images, statues and photographs of both men adorn the company's headquarters. He revered their memory daily, and was fully aware of their achievements, but he matched them in piety and philanthropy. Those who knew him are very willing to tell stories of his personal generosity.

His twin preoccupations had always been the management of the Peerless Group and the nurturing of his family. He was married to Shikha in 1973. Their son, Jayanta Roy, and daughter, Debasree Roy Sarkar, are both closely involved with the company's affairs.

S.K. Roy was a true visionary. He understood the business of small savings would not be feasible for future generations to run smoothly with regulatory norms and issues. His personal drive, charm and vision was one of the secrets of Peerless's survival.

He initiated the transformation of Peerless into a different business model altogether. To achieve this goal, he recruited the right people when he had to, garnered their support and raised enormous sums of money when he needed to.

The final phase of the remodelling of the Peerless Group into what it is today was therefore undertaken after 2011, when the RBI again made demands on the company, and required it to end its connection with small deposit holders. The entire asset base of certificate holder deposits was taken out of the company's control in 2014, and it was restricted to making final settlements on maturity. The original part of the company had by now become a relic – static and to some degree anachronistic, and the Peerless Group, under the leadership of S.K. Roy, diversified its business, most of which carried the Peerless brand.

Instead of dealing with small depositors in remote places, the modern Peerless group, with S.K. Roy at the helm of affairs, owned gleaming hospitals and luxurious hotels, and built modern housing units. It still employs thousands of people, and it still sells financial products to members of the public with small sums to dispose of. All the while, a sense of social responsibility, of a wider involvement with the health and well-being of its host community, was prominent within his leadership's priorities.

Once when S.K. Roy was asked to describe himself, without hesitation he replied, 'I am a simpleton.'[3] He liked to describe himself as a simpleton, but this was clearly not true of a man who, within ten years, turned an annual loss of more than ₹4,000 into regular profits, and who built up a net worth ₹12,140 crore. Simple in manner and outlook perhaps, but undoubtedly effective.

D.N. Ghosh has a clear understanding, 'S.K. Roy may not be hands-on in every job, but he had a unique quality of getting loyal people. Then he got them working as a team to get things done. That is a great quality.'[4]

Such a remark is tribute to the clarity of his outlook; he preferred to see things and do things in simple terms.

Professor A.K. Basu concurs. 'He was entirely approachable. I believe that his relations, his friends and even his employees could easily approach him, without the least inhibition ... Once in the course of a conversation, Mr Roy observed that he was proud of being the son of a schoolteacher. This pedigree has obviously enlightened Mr Roy with the sense of value and culture. Thus, even with his opulence and undeniable importance in the sphere of business in India, he contemptuously shuns snobbery and arrogance.' Professor Basu's overall impression of him is that he was 'out and out a people's man'.

S.K. Roy's own words were equally revealing. 'I saw that my brother laid more stress on recruiting people who were dedicated and with domain knowledge in their respective fields. He consciously avoided hiring those inclined to cut corners to reach their goals. This was in keeping with the overall philosophy of the company. It was this instinct and tradition that guided him after 1996 in his efforts to create a suitable leadership cadre to cope with the rapidly diversifying nature of the Peerless businesses.'

When asked how he envisioned the future of Peerless, S.K. Roy had a one-word reply. 'Unlimited.'[5]

The Guiding Light for Future

Braving quite a few serious medical ailments over several years, S.K. Roy passed away on 8 May 2022, leaving behind a vibrant legacy of trust, integrity and the wealth of spiritual fortitude. He had written, **'We continue to believe that, when the intentions are pure and the labour is honest, blessed are the fruits that accrue.'**

Such a faith was and is hard to shake in the presence of continued success.

P.P. Ray, President, Compliances and Legal, PGFI, has neatly both summarized and illustrated the Group's integrated philosophy of action. 'We have honoured the faith reposed in us. A fact whose vindication can be found in the near total absence of litigation faced by a group of this size and stature with so many varied lines of businesses and spread across geographical areas as we are. Our success and experience in Bengal Peerless Housing Development Company Limited, the first joint venture entered into by the West Bengal Housing Board, is also largely due to this practice of being totally compliant with the laws of the land – in letter and spirit.'[6]

Willing cooperation with the regulatory bodies, charitable distribution, the 'maturity melas' and advertising campaigns designed to encourage certificate holders to claim their pay-outs – all this has marked out the way Peerless has tried to take from and give back to individuals, society and the nation, and it intends to continue to do so.

That is the Peerless way.

The Road Ahead

The Roy family remains centrally involved with the company, which offers further continuity into the future. S.K. Roy's successors, Jayanta and Debasree, have been carefully mentored within the Peerless business environment. This lends a degree of security to the forward outlook. The successful formula that the Peerless Group has developed does not need to change, and it is hard to imagine why it would, or who would alter or abandon it.

But the times, they keep changing. The circumstances under which Jayanta Roy takes over the mantle are vastly different from the circumstances under which his illustrious father, S.K Roy took over the mantle from B.K. Roy. The world has become more digital. Employees have more opportunities and choices. Customers are better informed and empowered to make their choices. Businesses have become more connected. Resilience comes at a greater premium.

The road ahead may be fraught with challenges but the leadership under Jayanta Roy is replete with optimism and Peerless values.

Peerless has embarked upon a significant transformation journey to keep pace with the contemporary business environment, customer preferences and employee aspirations. Continuing the legacy of trust and contribution to society, the Group vision is 'to drive trust, profitable growth and pride of belonging for delivering sustainable stakeholder value.'

The healthcare segment will have primary focus, with an intention to grow in scale, profitability and sustainability. This will mean improvement in operating efficiencies, as well as increasing the footprint through a mix of organic and inorganic play.

One of the major projects currently underway is the extensive revamp and expansion of the Hospitex Hospital and B.K. Roy Research Centre. This further realizes the dream of B.K. Roy, and adds further possibilities for charitable activities and contributions to the benefit of national life. The hospitality business, headed by Debasree Roy Sarkar, will also go through a process of improvement and scale-up. The immediate task at hand will be to improve the operations of the hotels business and become a destination of choice for customers. Hotels business may also see material scale-up through partnerships.

The real estate business is another area of opportunity for Peerless. Having delivered high quality affordable residences through a joint venture with the West Bengal Housing Board (Bengal Peerless), Peerless may also explore the real estate business on its own, by leveraging the expertise gained from the Bengal Peerless operations.

With an increasing focus on performance and operational improvement primarily, the future of other businesses will depend on whether they can be profitably scaled up to a meaningful level.

The tradition of conducting business with a social impact will continue. Peerless initiated CSR activities during the floods in West Bengal in 1978. With B.K. Roy leading from the front, this philanthropic act was rooted in the firm belief of doing business beyond profits and touching common lives for betterment. The primary levers now will be the Peerless Skill Academy and the Gadadhar Abhyudaya Prakalpa, among others. The deep partnership of the Peerless Group with the Ramakrishna Mission will continue in all its strength under the present leadership.

What remains at the core of Peerless are the fundamental management practices of the past and present generations. Following the footsteps of his illustrious predecessors, Jayanta Roy has also concentrated on building the right team of talented professionals to transform and modernize Peerless with the changing times.

Jayanta Roy elaborates, 'From the very inception, our grandfather Radhashyam Roy emphasized proper governance. Even during the pre-Independence era, he professionalized a Board with the right set of like-minded, dedicated individuals. In pursuit of those same work ethics and principles, our father, S.K. Roy, inducted D.N. Ghosh, S.M. Dutta, D. Basu and others. Following the same path, we too have engaged ourselves in an active partnership between a seasoned professional and an enthusiastic promoter.'

A keen learner, Jayanta Roy is being ably guided by an august team of accomplished men from his father's time as well as newly inducted experts that includes Partha Sarathi Bhattacharya, former chairman of Coal India Limited, Arijit Basu, former managing director, SBI and Sumit Bose, former finance secretary, Government of India.

Jayanta Roy echoes his forefathers when he reiterates, 'Once the governance is right and the motive is beyond self, team members find their own purpose to seek and strive towards one common goal.'

At its heart, the Peerless saga remains an uplifting story of how a small local enterprise grew into a national corporation without losing its identity. The ideas of family, trust, service and nation that the company upholds are constantly traceable through the major episodes in its history, and remain ever present in its diverse activities. **For posterity, the only abiding law, it seems, is the integrity of karma and sevā – which is the core of 'being and becoming' peerless.**

Notes

Preface

1. R.M. Lala, *The Creation of Wealth: The Tatas from the 19th to the 21st Century*, Penguin, New Delhi, 2004.

2. The Founder

1. *Tattwamanjari* was started by Ram Chandra Dutta (30 October 1851–17 January 1899), a lay disciple of Sri Ramakrishna. He was also the founder of Ramakrishna Math (Yogodyan) in Kolkata.
2. *Sangha-janani*: The Mother of the Ramakrishna Movement.

3. The Beginning

1. A.K. Chatterjee, *A Peerless Education*, Calcutta, p. 332, f.n. 223, 1999.
2. Elder brother in Bengali.

3. *1932: The Symbol of Trust: The Peerless Journey*, The Indian Express, Howrah, p.29, 2017.
4. Ibid., p. 54.

4. The Architect

1. *1932: The Symbol of Trust*, p. 27.
2. Ibid., p. 29.
3. Ibid.
4. Dilip Roy (Ed.), *Strategic Management: Indian Experience*, Gyan Publishing, 1999.
5. *1932: The Symbol of Trust*, p. 27.
6. Interview by Roderick Mathews for *Being Peerless*, 3 July 2019.
7. Ibid.
8. Ibid.
9. PGFI, Chairman's Report, 2014.

6. Interregnum

1. T. Bandyopadhyay, *Sahara: The Untold Story*, Jaico Publishing Hourse, Mumbai, p. 45, 2014.
2. Interview by Roderick Mathews for *Being Peerless*, 3 July 2019.
3. Reserve Bank of India vs Peerless General Finance & Investment Co. Ltd. Ors. And Vice on 22 January, 1987, *Indian Kanoon*, https://indiankanoon.org/doc/1149874./.

7. New Protocols, New Experiments

1. Roy (Ed.), *Strategic Management*, p. 22.
2. Ibid., pp. 22–23.
3. Interview by Roderick Mathews for *Being Peerless*, 3 July 2019.
4. Roy (Ed.), *Strategic Management*, p. 23.
5. Ibid., p. 26.
6. Reserve Bank of India & Peerless General Finance and Investment Co. Ltd. And Anr. vs Reserve Bank Of India on 30 January, 1992, *Indian Kanoon*, https://indiankanoon.org/doc/1316639/.
7. Reserve Bank of India & Peerless General Finance and Investment Company Ltd. & Anr., *Indian Kanoon*, https://indiankanoon.org/doc/457553/.

8. The Turnaround

1. D.N. Ghosh, *No Regrets*, Rupa Publications, India, p. 341, 2015.
2. Interview by Roderick Mathews for *Being Peerless*, 4 July 2019.
3. Ibid.
4. Ibid.
5. Bandyopadhyay, Sahara: The Untold Story, p. 43.
6. Ibid.
7. Ibid.
8. Interview by Roderick Mathews for *Being Peerless*, 4 July 2019, 4 July 2019.

9. D.N. Ghosh, *No Regrets*, p. 344.
10. Ibid.
11. Ibid., p. 345.
12. Ibid., p. 344.
13. Ibid., p. 345.
14. PGFl Chairman's Speech, AGM, 30 September, 1996.
15. Interview by Roderick Mathews for *Being Peerless*, 4 July 2019.
16. Ibid.
17. D.N. Ghosh, Disciplining RNBCs, *Economic & Political Weekly*, Vol. 39, No. 18, 1 May 2004.
18. Interview by Roderick Mathews for *Being Peerless*, 4 July 2019.
19. Bandyopadhyay, *Sahara: The Untold Story*, p. 41.
20. D.N. Ghosh, *No Regrets*, p. 347.
21. T. Bandyopadhyay, *Sahara: The Untold Story*, p. 43.
22. D.N. Ghosh, *No Regrets*, p. 347.
23. T. Bandyopadhyay, *Sahara: The Untold Story*, p. 41.
24. D.N. Ghosh, *No Regrets*, p. 348.
25. Interview by Roderick Mathews for *Being Peerless*, 4 July 2019.
26. Atal Bihari Vajpayee, BJP Prime Minister, 1998–2004.
27. Interview by Roderick Mathews for *Being Peerless*, 3 July 2019.
28. D.N. Ghosh, *No Regrets*, p. 347.
29. Ibid., p. 346.
30. Ibid.
31. Ibid.

Notes

32. Ibid., p. 347.
33. Interview by Roderick Mathews for *Being Peerless*, 4 July 2019.
34. Interview by Roderick Mathews for *Being Peerless*, 4 July 2019.
35. Ghosh, *No Regrets*, p. 346.
36. Interview by Roderick Mathews for *Being Peerless*, 4 July 2019.
37. Ibid.
38. D.N. Ghosh, *No Regrets*, p. 350.
39. Ibid., p. 350.
40. Bandyopadhyay, *Sahara: The Untold Story*, p. 45.
41. PGFI Chairman's Speech, AGM, 29 November 2000.
42. PGFI Chairman's Speech, AGM, 29 November 2002.
43. PGFI Chairman's Speech, AGM, 22 September 2003.
44. PGFI Chairman's Speech, AGM, 31 August 2004.
45. V.Y. Reddy, *Advice and Dissent: My Life in Public Service*, HarperCollins Publishers, India. 2017, Kindle Edition.
46. 'RBI Hardens RNBC Investment Norms', *The Economic Times*, 23 June 2004.
47. D.N. Ghosh, *No Regrets*, p. 351.
48. PGFI Chairman's Speech, AGM, 19 August 2006.
49. Ibid.
50. Ibid.

9. Towards a New Model

1. PGFI Chairman's Speech, AGM, 14 September 2007.
2. Ibid.
3. Ibid.
4. Ibid.
5. Ibid.
6. PGFI, Chairman's Report, 2010.
7. PGFI, Chairman's Report, 2011.
8. 'Essel Finance Acquires Peerless Mutual Fund', *The Economic Times*, 10 November 2016.
9. *1932: The Symbol of Trust*, p. 25.
10. PGFI, Chairman's Report, 2014.
11 Ibid.
12. Times of India, 10 November 2016.
13. Interview by Roderick Mathews for *Being Peerless*, 3 July 2019.

10. The Guiding Light for Future

1. Elder brother.
2. *1932: The Symbol of Trust*, p. 26.
3. Interview by Roderick Mathews for *Being Peerless*, 8 January 2019.
4. Interview by Roderick Mathews for *Being Peerless*, 4 July 2019.
5. Interview by Roderick Mathews for *Being Peerless*, 2 July 2019.
6. *1932: The Symbol of Trust*, p.56.

"তরীখানি বাইতে গেলে
মাঝে মাঝে তুফান মেলে
তাই বলে হাল ছেড়ে দেওয়া
চলবে না ভাই চলবে না।"

*While rowing the boat we shall have to
brave the rough waves;
So, brother, we shall never retreat from
our onward movement.*

Shri B.K. Roy's oft-quoted lines, based on one of his favourite songs by Rabindranath Tagore, 'Aami bhoy korbo na bhoy korbo na' ('I shall not fear'), *Gitabitan Akhanda*, Visva Bharati Publications, 2015.